Notes to Stephanie:

Days Remembered

By

Jeffery W. Turner

Jeffery W. Turner

Copyright 2010 © Jeffery W. Turner

All rights reserved. No part of this publication may be reproduced or transmitted in any form or by any means, electronic or mechanical, including photocopy, recording, or any information storage and retrieval system, without permission in writing from the publisher.

Published in the USA

ISBN 978-0-615-40642-8

Notes to Stephanie: Days Remembered

Table of Contents

Foreword 10

The Perfect Day 16

Our First Day Married 19

Jeffery W. Turner

Your Halloween Stuff 22

Going to the Kimball 25

My Birthday in 2007 29

Toby the Cat 32

Trade Days at Weatherford 37

The Unity Church Bookstore 42

The Pool on the Roof 46

A Trip to Laredo 50

Yikes! It's Ike! 56

The Lady in the Car 62

The Flea Market and Charles 66

Our First Date 71

The Date in the Park 75

Seeing Mama Mia 78

I Love You 83

Eating Lunch Together 87

In The Game Room Together 90

Notes to Stephanie: Days Remembered

Our Wedding Day 94

The Battleship and the Bistro 99

Driving Around Lake Country 104

Bonds Ranch Road: The View of Forever 106

The Hill at Heritage 110

Painting the Bathrooms and Kitchen 114

Moving You In and Rearranging the House 116

Renewing Our Vows at Unity Church 118

Wedding Picture Day 122

Zestfest with Mom 125

Tommy's Hamburgers 129

Roof Repairs and Such 134

Winter Storm Damage 137

Smoking A Turkey With Your Son 141

Your Students Love You 145

Family Marriage Angst 148

Living at Two Houses 152

Talking to Mom to Straighten Things Out 155

When You Watched Me Mow 158

Talking About Marriage 160

Shopping at Saigon Taipei Market 163

Eating Daffy, Menudo, Tongue, and Grasshoppers, Too 166

Napping at the Symphony 171

Napping at the Symphony 171

Seeing Wicked at Fair Park 175

CERT Class: Starting to be Partners 177

Unity Church and Reverend Roach 180

The Day It Rained Green Chicken 183

Our First Thanksgiving 187

Our First Christmas and Thanksgiving with My Family 191

Bringing and Sending You Flowers 194

Dinners with the Kids 197

Notes to Stephanie: Days Remembered

Spending the Night at Mom's 200

Playing Disc Golf as a Family 202

Swimming in the Middle of the Night 205

The Watches You Gave Me 208

Knick Knacks and Such 211

Shopping For Clothes at Sears 214

Goodwill and Salvation Army: Adventures in Shopping 217

Moving the Kids Out of Your House 221

The Trips for Jane 224

The Lake Worth Albertsons 231

The Shoe Repair Guys: Mr. Holmes and Mr. Norrell 236

The Doll You Bought 240

King's and Crow's Liquor 244

Jane's Bad Grades, Roger's Good Grades 248

CPA and CFA: They Aren't Professional Designations 251

Touring the County Jail and Homicide
    Night 254

Buying our Wedding Rings 259

Loving in the Pool 263

Fun in Fredericksburg 266

The Bridge over I-35W at Heritage 269

Another View of Forever 272

We Like Luby's 277

Driving Through Riverside 282

Tornado Sirens in the Dark 285

The Kid Working Alone 290

Your Little Classroom 294

Coco and Chocolate 297

Peach Ice Cream on 281 301

Winscot Road 303

Sunset Picnic in Aransas Park 307

I Wish We Had 310

Notes to Stephanie: Days Remembered

Do You Remember? 315

Afterword 323

Jeffery W. Turner

Foreword

After writing *Notes to Stephanie: Middle Aged Love Letters and Life Stories* (*NTS*), I thought I could never write a sequel to that book since there were no more notes that I had written to "Stephanie."

But on the afternoon of what would have been our

anniversary, I had a new idea. That new idea was to recount in some detail a particular day in our lives together and its events as if I was writing about them to her now. Unlike many of the notes in *NTS*, many of these stories are tales of the good days we had, although if I thought the day in question had some significance or there was a message about life to be told, I included it in this sequel. Some of the stories cover things that are mentioned or alluded to in *NTS* as well.

Also, I have not assigned dates to the notes in this book since I do not remember the exact dates of them in some cases. So when you read them, they are in the order I thought of them on the afternoon mentioned above. I simply scribbled the titles of the notes in my notepad in my car while I sat on a hill, watching the weather go by. Thus, they can be considered a "stream of consciousness" in some ways. As a result, many of them are not related to one another, even though there is some grouping of similar events and themes.

Why did I decide to do this? Many books have a sequel, which are sometimes meaningless with no real point or story; but I wanted mine to be different. There had to be a real reason for writing a second volume of *Notes*. The point of this book is to show we did have good days and times as opposed to the darker tone of *NTS*. But there is some sadness in these *Notes,* too; you will see that when you are reading about these events in our lives. However, that is the nature of life as I have written about before. Regardless, a different light is shined upon the story of our life together. Also, they say an author should write about what he knows. Since I lived these events, I know them well. That is the other reason for writing this book.

Notes to Stephanie: Days Remembered

As I wrote these new notes, they filled me with memories—some of which I had forgotten. When I wrote, I remembered them as vividly as if they had just happened. And thus the title of this book was born: *Notes to Stephanie: Days Remembered.* Therefore, this book is a memoir of sorts as opposed to the material in *NTS*, which I wrote as things happened between Stephanie and me.

When you read this book and its notes, I hope it makes you think of special days you had with someone you love or once loved. Especially the happy days—since those are the times we want to keep alive in our hearts and minds—and not the days that showed us things were not going to have a happy ending like a fairy tale always does.

But we all want a happy ending to our story when we are with someone we love, wishing that love would never end. In a way, singer Todd Rundgren sums this feeling up in his song "Fade Away": *"We must go on go on forever. The seas will rise, the mountains fall, the earth will turn itself upside down. But we have seen it all before, we will always be around. In a hundred million years, when the planet disappears, you and I will stay and watch the world fade away. And in a million, trillion years when the stars all disappear, you and I will stay and watch it all fade away."*

While those haunting and ethereal words are a wonderful vision of eternal love set against images of life's changes that state of affairs doesn't usually happen. Thus, life is always filled with a series of yin and yang moments. Happiness is matched with disappointment time and time again. The ups and downs of life are always around us and are something none of us can escape as long as we exist.

Notes to Stephanie: Days Remembered

But like the author of a fairy tale, we keep hoping that we will get our glass slipper one day, put it on, and live happily ever after with our special prince or princess to the end of time. I certainly did, and I guess I still do; but being a realist, I don't live my life around the likelihood of that taking place. But who knows what will happen, right? Maybe I will meet someone special whom I will write *Notes* to one day, telling the story of a new life and love in some unforeseen time.

Perhaps that hope for a new and better day is kept alive in our hearts by the images of days past. Thus, these "Days Remembered" provide the framework for our lives and what we hope for in the future.

Jeffery W. Turner, 5/5/2010.

Visit **www.ilypants.net** for more information.

Jeffery W. Turner

The Perfect Day

Do you remember the day we finished the French drain in the backyard by the pool? You did most of the work digging the trench that first June of our married life. With a large rainstorm looming, we had to finish the project to see if the drain worked. So, we decided that day was the day to get it done.

And so, we did. That day was like many June days. It was cloudy, humid, and windy. The radar showed the heavy rain was coming in, so we rushed to get the trench filled and smoothed over before the deluge hit us.

So, there we both were: me in my swimsuit and you in your light green bikini, looking sexy indeed. As we shoveled the dirt, we both got covered with mud from head to toe. But that was part of the fun, you see—working together to finish that important task under the threat of more rain to come.

Then, it started raining on us. We had a couple of beers and kept moving dirt as the rain fell. We finally got the ditch filled when the bottom fell out of the grey sky, and a long downpour was upon us and the earth.

But the pouring rain was a good thing. It cooled us off and also washed off all of the mud, grass, and sweat. Do you remember standing up in the rain as if it were a shower, laughing at that as we chugged on some beer? Since there was no lightning about, we just enjoyed being out in the cooling rain, getting clean and a little drunk at the same time.

We were out there awhile, and then the rain let up; and we went back inside and took a real shower. The rest of the day we relaxed, satisfied that the drain was diverting the water and working well. We were happy about taking a shower outside in the rain with a cold beer in our hands to wash away the dirt covering us both.

Certainly, that day was a perfect day. We did something as a couple and really enjoyed it from start to finish. A day filled with work was also filled with fun and love together in the pouring rain on a warm summer day in June in the backyard by the pool.

Our First Day Married

I remember waking up the morning after we got married in my bedroom with you. We had survived the evening with our kids and the dinner after the wedding. The dinner had been great at Texas De Brazil; and we had gone to my house and loved on each other and fell asleep exhausted in each other's arms.

This first day as husband and wife was anticlimactic to the wedding. We both took the day off from work since we married midweek and did not go on a honeymoon. We simply did nothing much at all that day. The thing I remember the most was driving out to Weatherford that afternoon where you visited that MLS office you had been a member of. I recall that the day was bright, sunny, and warm.

We piled in one of the vehicles, and we went west on I-820 and I-20 to get there. Going to the MLS office did not take long, and we drove back to Fort Worth and my house.

We did not do much that night either as I recall. We talked about stuff like the houses and what we might do that coming weekend. We also talked about our upcoming wedding party and the invitations and wedding announcements I had mailed out, along with our private label hot sauce, "Together And Hot On Life," from Old Gringo Chile Company. I had finished that task the morning of our wedding before my kids came over.

Certainly, it was a quiet and peaceful day. Too bad we did not know what was about to hit us from our families since we hadn't told them we were getting hitched. That wrenching series of events was a good lesson in life. What you think may be harmless and cute may in fact be perceived as the total opposite. Sometimes, we as human beings get wrapped up in our own plans and forget they may not be seen as innocently as we think. That quiet day was the opposite of what was about to come. In any event, we survived that, too; and to this day, I still have four bottles of the hot sauce. Even though you are gone, the picture of us on the label certainly brings back memories. And the hot sauce still tastes good just like the memories of our first day married.

Jeffery W. Turner

Your Halloween Stuff

Just the other Sunday, the day after Halloween, I went in the garage to get ready to mow the yard. After all of the rain, it was finally dry enough to do that and not be in a swamp or sea of mud.

After I filled up the mower with gas and pushed it out to the yard, I started looking at the stuff in the boxes you had left when you moved out. There was one large box filled with all of the Halloween decorations you bought or had when we met.

There were paper banners and little stuffed scarecrows, other Halloween figures, and wreaths for the door. There were several plastic pumpkins as well. And that was what got my attention more than anything, especially two of them. The two I am talking about were not your standard round variety but instead were tall and twisted with gnarly noses sticking out from their faces. I remembered how you would stick them out on the front porch—pumpkins on either side of the door.. But those two being different always stood out to me.

When I looked at them, they appeared sad in a way. Once they had made you and me happy, when you used them to decorate our house; but now they sat unused in a box never to adorn a home again. You had left them in that box, and I would not use them since I never decorated the house for any holiday except Christmas. Since I was also taking out the trash and cleaning some of the stuff you had left, I looked at the Halloween stuff and felt all of that had to go.

So, with a few tears in my eyes, I loaded all of those Halloween knick knacks into the trash bin and sat it out by the street under the shade trees. The two gnarly pumpkins were on the top—their empty gaze looking up to the sky as I closed the lid on them. I did not know why that made me so sad, but it did. I thought about getting them out of the trash can, but I didn't do that. So as you left them in the garage, I left them in the trash to be picked up and taken to the dump to be buried—never to be seen again, unless dug up one day for some unknown reason in some future neither of us would likely see.

But I will always remember those Halloweens with you, those two pumpkins on the porch, and how they brought life to our house at that time of the year. So in a way, those two pumpkins will still bring a treat, not a trick, to my heart over time and the years to come.

Going to the Kimball

We went to the Kimball Museum more than once. Both of us liked art and enjoyed going to Fort Worth's museum district to visit the Kimball and the Amon Carter, which was my favorite.

I am not some art "nut," but I do like looking at pictures. Having good art myself, something other than pictures of sports or girls in bikinis, I appreciated and enjoyed looking at works by great and famous artists.

The exhibit I remember the most seeing with you was the impressionist show. Works by Monet, Van Gogh, and others adorned the walls of the museum with their splendor. I always liked art like that since it reminded me of abstract painting, which my mom had when I grew up. The soft colors and less defined shapes gave those paintings a dreamlike quality, which always appealed to me.

We went to the Kimball that Sunday with throngs of other art lovers to see the works inside. We walked from picture to picture and gazed at them all. You were wearing a pair of the headphones the museum rented out, which played a recording explaining the paintings. As we walked by one framed image, you repeated to me some of what they were saying on the recordings. We took a bit more than an hour to look at them all, not lingering on a particular painting like some of the patrons did. Even though our time there was short, it was fun and refreshing to see the works.

Notes to Stephanie: Days Remembered

After the Kimball, we went downtown to the Flying Saucer, had a couple of beers, and sat and talked about stuff going on. We strolled around Sundance Square and went into the Sid Richardson gallery to look at their western art since we did not go to the Amon Carter that day. Couldn't forget those Remingtons and Russells, could we? After awhile there, we were ready to go home and call it a day. We drove back to the house—our minds filled with images of great paintings of the masters of the past.

That day was very good with you. It was a fun and intellectual time together. We did things like that more than once since you and I did have that in common. These were things sometimes not well liked by the mainstream, however. We were a little different than most folks in that way. Our hobbies and life philosophies were sometimes out on the edge of the bell curve of possibilities, but neither of us ever had an issue with that. The interests we had sometimes were the same; and when they were not, at least we could appreciate what the other liked or thought.

Some couples argue about things like hobbies or what to watch on TV, but we never did that. Instead, we argued about other things that in the end hurt us both. We should have remembered the times we had at places like the Kimball. Both of us should have strived to imitate the grace and beauty in the museum pictures in our own life together. If we had done that, the canvas of our memories would have been painted with far brighter colors than they were in the end.

Notes to Stephanie: Days Remembered

My Birthday in 2007

Even now, I can truly say one of my best adult birthdays was in 2007 with you. You did something a little unusual for me that day. The big part of the day was going to the Museum of Natural History to see a show at its IMAX theatre. In my whole life, I had never seen one of those shows, and it was quite neat. I remember sitting in the seats, which curved around the theatre, watching the huge screen with you there next to me. Seeing that IMAX movie made me want to see more like that—we just never did that unfortunately.

After the show, we walked around the museum. That was fun, and it brought back many childhood memories of going there with my parents. The exhibits were filled with kids and their parents walking around looking at or interacting with the exhibits they saw. Such a museum is a great place for families, for sure, or couples like we were.

That May day was cool and a bit rainy. I remember sitting on that second story area with you, having a snack to raise my low blood sugar. We watched the rain drip down onto the rocks, trees, and plants below us in the atrium that had some turtles swimming around in a pool. We both thought it was peaceful and pretty all at the same time.

The grey skies did not darken things that day either. The cool temperatures and rain were an added blessing to a day that you made so special for me. All birthdays should be that way for everyone. They should never be ruined by someone else who does something to annoy you or make you mad. While birthdays get more routine and maybe even meaningless as you get older, I really loved that day. You made it a fun, unique, and all around good day. A wonderful time that, among all of my birthdays, I will always remember with good and cherished thoughts. Such memories are perhaps the best present that a person can ever be given by someone they loved.

Toby the Cat

When we were kids did you watch Felix the Cat? Do you remember the lyrics to his carton theme?

"Felix the Cat, the wonderful, wonderful cat,

Whenever he gets in a fix, he reaches into his bag of tricks.

You'll laugh so much your sides will ache,

Your heart will go pitter pat,

Watching Felix, the wonderful cat."

In our case, the name of the wonderful, wonderful cat was not Felix but was Toby

Notes to Stephanie: Days Remembered

"Tobias" Turner. Yes, Toby it was. In your efforts to fight the empty nest syndrome, you finally convinced me to get a pet—a cat, specifically—since I did not want a dog in the house and don't really like most dogs. Thus, finding a kitten was an answer to your needs. It was also a good compromise between us since I never had a pet when I was single.

So one Saturday, you went down the street to the nearby animal shelter. You brought home a beautiful, little, grey, striped, male kitten. His stripes were unusual and very striking: he would grow up into a very nice looking tom cat. You named him Toby at the shelter, even as other people were also thinking about getting him. You said, however, that you had never had tom cats before, only mama cats; and while you thought he was lovely, you were concerned about some of his future adult habits like marking his territory. You were certainly wrong on that fear as we all saw him grow up into a very good adult tom cat.

When you got home with him, he was, of course, hesitant about his new, unknown place of residence. But he warmed up to us pretty quickly. I remember the first night he was there, and we put him in the bed with us—on a towel between us in case he had some accident and to keep him warm. In the morning, he was still there where we put him, seemingly comfortable and at ease. That pattern continued as he never strayed far from us even when he was grown. While not a lap cat, he was loving and affectionate all the same. While sometimes aloof like many cats, he usually liked being part of what we were doing.

He loved us both, but over time, I seemed to become his favorite. When I was in my recliner at night, he would jump on top of the chair and just sit there behind my head, content as I rocked and watched TV with you. In the morning when I got up, he would follow me into the kitchen and jump on the counter to watch what I was doing. And best of all, you always said he would go to the front door and meow and whine when I left before you. He did love you, too, but I was perhaps his parent. At least, that is what you thought he was doing. Maybe so, but that is how he behaved.

While he loved us both, he also did not know what it was like to be a cat. That is until your son moved in with us and brought his cat, Slinkster, with him. Those two cats fought some; but in the end, they learned to peacefully coexist with one another. A feline détente, if you will. One thing I saw in Toby was that after The Slink was around, he was a bit more aloof and independent than he was before, which is the way most cats are anyway. But that was okay since his other good habits remained, such as his affectionate nature and his desire to be around us. He always was that way with all of us, including the kids.

In retrospect, he was the best cat I ever had. I trust to this day that he acts the same way and is a fat, happy, and content tom cat. That is how it should be for a wonderful, wonderful cat named Toby, who was loved by all and also loved his family. I will never forget him and how happy he made me feel.

Notes to Stephanie: Days Remembered

Trade Days at Weatherford

The day we went to the trade days at Weatherford was a fun day. You had spoken about how you and your kids had gone there over the years and how much fun it was. And, of course, you were seeking "junk" as you did at the flea market at Will Rogers. So, going there sounded okay to me.

One Saturday, we climbed in the truck and headed west on I-20 to Parker County and Weatherford. There was a bit of traffic when we got into town—other folks trying to get there, too. We drove around to one side of the fairgrounds, where the trade days were held and walked into the fray.

The place covered a few acres but was not full. You remarked on how much busier it had been in past years. I replied that with the economy slowing down, folks did not have the extra income to spend on the stuff that was usually sold at places like this. Junk to me, but certainly not junk to others. Regardless, it was not busy.

Besides the usual cheap, plastic items from China or elsewhere, there were a couple of things that did catch our eye that sunny day. The first were those handmade, metal western-style lamps. Of course, that was when we still were going to redo the kitchen in a western style. Even though the bedroom was where the lamps would have gone, we still liked them, (although the bedroom would stay non-western). We did not buy them for some reason, and we walked through more stalls to see what they had.

Notes to Stephanie: Days Remembered

The second interesting thing that we saw we actually bought. This was the jar of honey from the guy whom I think lived up by Wichita Falls or Vernon. You liked the variety he had, and we bought a single jar, which we took with us. That jar of honey is still in my pantry, by the way, but I never eat any of it. And we walked up and down the paths lined with all types of stuff we did not need or want.

After a couple of hours wandering around the place looking at stuff no one was buying, we got back in the truck, headed east, and stopped at the Mesquite Pit for lunch. Years ago, I had eaten there.

The Pit is a restaurant one could use as an example of a typical Texas country dining establishment. It has BBQ, chicken fried steak, and hamburgers. It has few items on its menu that would appeal to a member of PETA. Thankfully so, I might add.

We ordered and our food arrived, which we ate with some gusto. While the food was good, the highlight of the meal was the peach daiquiris. Since the Weatherford area is known for its peaches, it was only right that they had such an adult beverage. The peach crops had not been good in recent years, so who knew where the peaches had come from? But the drink itself was refreshing and good since you could really taste the peaches. And thus, we drank two each and became pretty mellowed out.

But any good day must draw to its close, so we paid our tab and drove back to Fort Worth with full tummies and a slight buzz from the daiquiris. It was a fun day filled with more than one good thing—a jar of honey, some good chicken fried steak, a good drink, and of course, viewing the wide panoply of humanity at the trade days along with the seemingly endless sea of junk.

Certainly, we should all hope to have such days filled with simple and good things that are in contrast to our hectic, and sometimes, frustrating lives. Going to the trade days was one such day for sure.

Jeffery W. Turner

The Unity Church Bookstore

I always enjoyed going to the Fort Worth Unity Church and hearing Reverend Roach and his messages to the congregation. The Sundays there were always a pleasure. The friendly atmosphere of that church and the way the sermons appealed to one's intellect as well as one's spirituality was a combination that worked for us both.

Now, both of us never blindly followed the more orthodox ways of the fundamentalist church we were both raised and baptized in. The churches from our childhoods and Unity Church were in many ways opposite of each other—their sets of doctrines have little commonality. As one example, Unity's use of phrases like "Father/Mother/God" would certainly curdle the religious cheese of many who attended our former churches and others like it. The many diverse beliefs of the Unity movement were not for everyone.

Also, neither of us believed all that Unity taught either. Indeed, one of Unity's beliefs is that you don't have to believe everything they teach. Thus, their door is open to those who are religious, spiritual, or even atheist.

When we went into the bookstore at the Unity Church, we saw this same wide range of thinking on its shelves. During our time together, we both bought books and other items there. Those purchases helped the church, but also helped us by giving us something new to think about.

Each time we went inside the bookstore, there was something new to pick up and look at.

Some of the books and tapes were a bit out there for our tastes, but many were of great interest. My favorite was the book comparing the words and ideas of Jesus to Buddha. And there were others as well—for both of us. Not to mention, there were the interesting, handmade clothes that they also sold, which you sometimes bought, too.

In the end, that neat little store and its wide variety of products were like the church and its members— a cross section of people with a variety of beliefs and lifestyles but united by a set of values that everyone who attended shared. This was all illustrated by the different types of books and other items on the shelves of the bookstore. That store was small in size, but it was very large in the stock of ideas that it made available to those who entered its friendly doors.

All groups, whether religious or not, should afford everyone that same gentle social tone and the ability to retain one's own beliefs all while one's intellect is nourished along with the soul.

The Pool on the Roof

Another day I fondly remember is the day we stayed in San Antonio on the way back to Fort Worth from Laredo. As you know, I never liked Laredo itself much, but San Antonio was a place I enjoyed. So being able to spend a little time there was something I looked forward to.

After leaving Laredo and arriving in The Alamo City, I was pleased with the hotel we chose to stay in. The room was nice, and the place was convenient to the River Walk along with being close to the Mercado and the famous Mi Tierra restaurant. But my favorite thing was the swimming pool on the roof of the place. "A pool with a view," one might say, tweaking the old phrase about a room with a view.

So to relax before having dinner some place on the River Walk, we put on our swimming suits, grabbed a towel, and took the elevator up to the top of the building.

Up there we could see the sweep of the city and the hill country to the west. The city itself was laid out around us, nestled between the hills sloping up to the west. The day was bright and sunny with some high clouds strewn above us, flowing from the southwest. It was a bit hot, but what day in the Texas summer isn't? At least the humidity was low. There were people there with their kids, other couples, and some folks not so attached. The water was cool as I remember, and we jumped in.

The Jacuzzi was going, too, and its jets felt good after the drive from the Rio Grande that morning. I remember looking around at the city and you again. You seemed to be at ease, which was something I had wondered about, since the city we were in was where the people, who adopted you when you were a little girl, tried to kill you. I wondered what was going through your mind sometimes when you looked out in silence at the view stretching to the horizon. Were you thinking about that nightmare or something else like the winter day you were in downtown in the cold and managed to get a cup of hot cocoa? I did not ask you what you were thinking since the people around us did not need to know about those things. The day was so wonderful; bringing up the past pain might have spoiled the moment and caused you hurt, so I kept those thoughts to myself.

But that tells us something, doesn't it? Most places where we might go are filled with reminders of the past. Some are good and some are bad. But they are there, regardless of how they might make us feel. We can be driving down the street and something we see reminds us of one of those times. We can be most anywhere, and these thoughts will surface from the depths of our personal memories. Not going to places where these thoughts lurk is impossible since they are everywhere. Staying away from memories and the places they come from is never possible to do. Thus, if we never went to places or experienced new things, we wouldn't be living after all. The memories, whether good or bad, found on any given day and at any place are the costs and benefits of being alive. And that day on top of a building in San Antonio in a swimming pool with you was one of those wonderful days that provided me with a set of good memories that are still with me today.

Jeffery W. Turner

A Trip to Laredo

Laredo, Laredo. Laredo. It seemed it was your favorite place on earth to visit. For most of your adult years, you had gone there and also Nuevo Laredo across the Rio Grande. You were enthralled with the city and its Mexican sister. However, I was not so enthralled with it, but I went with you there because you liked it.

Yes, I should not be critical of the place per se since like all cities and towns, it had something that drew folks to it and made its natives stay there for lifetimes or return to it at some point to live once more. Like many border areas, it certainly had a split personality. One side of the river, you had a pretty typical American town with an interstate, a mall, and the usual things like grocery stores, churches, and houses. However, across the Rio Grande, you could see the usual squalor of a Mexican border town, filled with shops for the tourists, people trying to sell you stuff, and other modern oddities like the many pharmacies—most of which prey on the unwary gringos who were looking for cheap medicine or medical treatments. Thus, the area truly had two opposite sides.

Preferring the American way of doing things, I never felt comfortable across the river and certainly did not enjoy being over there. Being bilingual, you certainly were more comfortable there even though you were wary of possible miscreants around us. But what really got me thinking about never going there again was the day we were there and the *Ejercito Mexicano* lined the main drag. The Mexican Regular Army was there.

Do you remember me asking the soldier in my bad Spanish if he was regular army or not? He said he was as he had his assault rifle slung over his shoulder. The Mexican Army was standing there with Hummers and "Deuce and a Halves" as a result of the drug cartel wars, which had spilled onto the streets of Nuevo Laredo, resulting in murder and mayhem. The Mexican government brought in their Army and Federal Police, the so-called *Federales*, to calm things down. Gunfire or the threat of it was bad for tourism. Regardless of the effects, light infantry forces on Main Street were not a good thing for *Norte Americanos* to see if you wanted lots of them to cross the bridge and buy stuff at the Mercado on Guererro.

And on top of that, do you remember the U.S. Army OH-58D Kiowa Warrior scout helicopter hovering on the U.S. side with its front pointed toward the Mexican side? This was not just some helicopter that flew around for no reason. But it was the type with a "spy ball" on top of the rotor and with targeting lasers that would have been used to paint a vehicle so it could have been blasted by some guided munition, like a 155MM Copperhead artillery round or Hellfire missile. It seemed we were sending some unofficial message to the folks on the Mexican side with its presence. Their military knew what was hovering across the river. Don't think they didn't.

The whole situation that day did not make me feel like going back there. You did not think it was that major, especially since your family friend Dr. Rubio told us it was not that big of a deal. Well, regardless of what the good and respected doctor said, having military on the streets to help police the place is not a good thing. And don't forget the *Federales* were also out in their grey uniforms, riding around in black pickups with their military grade rifles visible.

In short, there were some interesting and good things about Laredo and even Nuevo Laredo, but I never felt at ease when we were across the river. Certainly, that shows that a place can be interesting and even beautiful to one person but the complete opposite to someone else. This proves the old saying that beauty is in the eye of the beholder. Indeed the Laredo/Nuevo Laredo area, called El Dos Laredos by some, was a place that you thought had beauty and art—seen in its streets, neighborhoods, and people. Even the poverty and squalor on the Mexican side had some intrinsic quality that appealed to you. I, of course, saw mostly the opposite even though Laredo, Texas itself was not a bad place.

I guess that tells the story of whom we both are in some ways, doesn't it? You saw one thing in a place, and I saw something totally different. You saw something positive in the decay and poverty, and I saw the squalor itself without some redeeming, artistic quality. You saw the rainbow, and I saw the black and white.

This dichotomy also confirms another old saying. The one that says it takes all kinds of people to make the world go around. And so it does, and so it was with us on the streets of Laredo that spring day.

Jeffery W. Turner

Yikes! It's Ike!

While we were members of CERT (Community Emergency Response Team), we never had a disaster in our area where we were called up to help the fire or police department. But that changed when Hurricane Ike slammed into Galveston and Houston. At first, nothing happened that affected us except for my daughter Jane fleeing Galveston. But then, we were contacted by Officer Monty Lambert; and we knew we were being called up to help.

We were told to assemble at that Fort Worth ISD sports facility near the college north of I-20 that Sunday evening to help dispense drinks and snacks from the Red Cross to busloads of refugees coming into the area. We drove down there and joined the CERT members . There were some Fort Worth police officers and a TV crew. So, we stood around with our CERT vests on and waited for the buses to show up. Monty was talking on his radio and then came over to address us. He said the buses were near Fort Worth and would be arriving in groups or singly. Then we braced ourselves for the arrival of the fleet of buses, not knowing exactly what to expect.

And they started coming in. We divided up into teams of two—one team for each bus—and climbed aboard the buses filled to the brim with people from the coast, all tired and a bit grumpy. We walked down the aisles, passing out the cold water and handing out bags of chips or cookies to the adults and children in each seat. A few thanked us and a few complained about the limited selection of snacks. We simply said they would soon be at a real shelter where there would be meals and more drinks. We stepped out of the buses, which soon left for their final destinations. The TV crew never came over to see any of this. I guess there was not enough drama for this to get on the news.

After awhile of handing out the drinks and snacks, it became apparent that the Red Cross supplies had almost been exhausted. Someone would have to go to the Red Cross HQ near downtown to get more for the next batch of buses, which was coming from East Texas and bringing the refugees from a shelter that itself had to be evacuated due to storm damage. Monty started seeking volunteers, and we stepped forward since we had a truck, which could carry a large amount of supplies.

We climbed in the truck and followed the man from the Red Cross to their HQ on Riverside, east of downtown.

Inside the building, there was a scene of controlled chaos. The staff of the Red Cross was busy getting shelters set up, staffed, and supplies staged to the many locations scattered across the region around Fort Worth. We soon learned that supplies were scarce, but we did get some. We loaded up the truck and returned back to the bus staging area, unloading it for the next group of displaced citizens.

Later, more buses came by filled with tired and dazed people who simply wanted a place to be comfortable and get a hot meal. We handed out water and chips again to similar thanks and gripes as before. We left for home when the overnight shift came on to relieve us, and we were done for the day.

During the work week, we were not needed; but the next weekend we were called up again to staff the Emergency HQ at the Police Academy. That day was anticlimactic compared to the previous weekend. We just answered a few phone calls and forwarded messages to the Fort Worth emergency management staff, who were in the room with us. No more buses filled with tired and griping people or scurrying around to find more supplies. We just sat in a big and mostly empty auditorium, which was normally used for classes, and relayed information from one group to another.

And yet our mundane efforts that second weekend did affect the masses of refugees without us seeing the actual results of our work.

In fact, that is the lesson to be drawn from those two weekends. There is more than one way to help those who need our help. You can do something hands-on like go on a crowded bus, or you can work behind the scenes where no one will ever know whom you are or what you did. You don't have to give a lot of money or be in the public eye to help out your fellow man, but at least make the effort, even in a small way, to help someone else from time to time. Who knows? The next time something bad happens, you might be one of the people on the bus looking for a drink and a snack from someone you don't know.

Jeffery W. Turner

The Lady in the Car

One Sunday, we went driving around the west side of Lake Worth and also to Lake Country as you liked to do many times. In that sense, that little trip was no different than others we had done, but that Sunday would be unlike the others.

We left the Lake Country area and went to a new housing development via some back roads overlooking the south end of Eagle Mountain Lake. Next, we turned into the place where you wanted to go, which was an area with large lots that stair-stepped up a hill to the east of the road.

We drove slowly up the street, looking at the empty lots until we got to the top of the hill and stopped. We slurped down a beer or two and looked down the hill at the terrain, trying to guess what the price per lot was. We saw a couple of cars go by, then left that spot, and drove to the development next to that one.

That tract was more developed since it had several finished homes on it. It was adjacent to an older "bread and butter" neighborhood you were familiar with from your real estate days. We drove slowly down the street, which went south, and then turned around and came back.

As we passed a house, we went by a car with a lady in its front seat. She looked like she was asleep. We wondered about her; we thought perhaps something was wrong with her, so we turned back around and parked the truck in front of her car. She did not move or notice our arrival, and our fears were fueled by her lack of movement.

We got out and looked in at her. She was out like a light it seemed. Before calling 911, we knocked on the windows pretty hard to see if she would wake up. And to our surprise and relief, she did jerk up.

We asked her if she was okay as she rolled down her window—still a little groggy. We asked her again if she was well and explained what we had seen. She said she was looking at houses, too, and she had simply dozed off in her car. It was a warm day, so that seemed logical to us. We ended the conversation and left her and that neighborhood for home.

That Sunday afternoon was more than just a joy ride, looking for a house for us. It also showed we could think about and care for other people. For a moment, we were good Samaritans who were at the right place and time to help someone. In this age, how many people would have simply kept driving, thinking they did not want to get involved? Or simply said, "It's not my problem"? Probably a lot of our fellow citizens would have done just that.

It is a shame that people cannot, even for a moment, divorce themselves from their own interests to simply see if they could help another person who might not be able to help himself. We can't vouch for others, but we certainly took a chance and asked if we could help someone we did not know. Others should do that, too, since you never know when the day will come when you might be the lady in the car and really need someone's help.

Jeffery W. Turner

The Flea Market and Charles

The Will Rogers Flea Market was one of those "good old places" in Fort Worth that you and I visited many times. Well, good for you, since going through the seemingly endless rows of junk was never my favorite thing to do. But you liked it, and we combined that activity with lunch or going to the Flying Saucer for a beer or two on our way home.

Walking down the aisles of the livestock barn where the flea market was located, one saw a strange array of things such as old household goods, collectibles, and junk better off at the dump. But occasionally there was a shining jewel among the mostly dull and useless refuse that was there. One such treasure was meeting Charles and buying his dead wife's cherished beading supplies. It was a stroke of good fortune since the beading supplies had value, especially the real turquoise pieces, which he sold to you for pennies on the dollar. And it was a wonderful event, too, since Charles was a good man and pleasant to be around each time we went to Will Rogers.

Certainly, he was kind by giving us such a good deal on what was left of his wife's earthly treasures. But what struck me most about him was how he remembered his wife. Like a lot of people, he had been married to his wife for many years and was shaken by her death. You could tell he missed her deeply; and at the same time, he carried himself upright through life, tending to his daughter and grandson, who he also dearly loved. And if I remember correctly, he said he had a slowly progressing terminal disease as well. But even with these hard things in his life, he always had a good outlook on things and was friendly every time we saw him.

His kindness to us, two people he hardly knew and owed nothing, was an exception compared to some in that flea market, who tried to sell you junk or outright cheat you. Selling his wife's beads was also as much an act of remembering her as it was selling goods he no longer needed to keep. He said he hoped you would enjoy the beads as much as his wife had. He seemed happy to see the excitement in your eyes as you beheld the riches in your hands, just as he could still see his beloved wife doing.

The many pieces of jewelry you made did give you pleasure. You made your fellow teachers guess where you got them. You never told how you made the sets of earrings and bracelets or the story behind what you crafted and wore. You see, by using her beads, you honored Charles and his wife. Your work with those little trinkets and stones made her live on just as she did in Charles's mind. So when you strung one of those beads, you did it in honor of his wife, whom he still deeply loved, and also in honor of the good man he was.

You can now see that Charles made an impression on us in more than one way. Seeing him was always a pleasure, but it was something we took for granted. We thought he would always be there, just like the old livestock barns at Will Rogers never seemed to change. But one day he left; his market stall was no more. He moved to Houston with his daughter, departing from the flea market and our lives. We wanted to contact him, thanking him once more; but he left no forwarding address with anyone there and was gone.

Indeed, he departed; but like the memories of his wife, who he loved and longed for so, the memory of him is still inside me. It makes me smile, feel a little sad, and wish he is well each time it appears. Hopefully one day, we will be remembered the same way by people we were kind to, just as Charles from the flea market is now by me.

Notes to Stephanie: Days Remembered

Our First Date

As we were getting divorced, you once e-mailed me that you would always remember our first date. While I have not forgotten it either, I do not get sentimental about it. But it was a very wonderful evening, and that is what I will recount below.

I remember you came over to my house, and you rang the door bell. There you were in the pretty greenish dress that fit you so well; your legs looked great, as did your hair. We talked a little, I showed you my house, and we got in my truck and headed out for dinner.

I remember talking about various things like our life histories as we drove south to Haltom City and the Thai restaurant I had picked out. You and I liked more than one type of food, and that was one of the biggest things that first attracted me to you.

We got to the Thai place and went in, sitting towards the front of the place, which was not crowded at all. I think I had a hot green curry dish, and we had Thai beef salad as an appetizer. It was all good, and the meal hit the spot. Our conversation, of course, continued.

After that we drove downtown to Sundance Square and wandered around, we finally ended up at Billy Miner's Saloon where I had eaten lunch years before when I worked downtown. We had some drinks and talked some more. One thing that was interesting was that a lot of people gazed at us through the window as they walked by—one guy in particular as I recall. Were they gazing at you or were they gazing at us together since we were so enthralled with each other? Who knows? They looked at us—that is for sure.

Regardless of the people looking at us, we also looked at each other throughout the evening. The night went on that way until we left to go back to my house. When we got back to my place, we got out of my truck, had a little good night kiss, and said we wanted to go out again—our arms around each other. We said goodbye, left, and I went back inside thinking about the night. *It was a good first date,* I thought. And my gut told me the same thing, too.

That humid summer night in July was our official beginning as a couple. I wish we had found a way to keep that interest alive and had not stopped looking into each other's eyes, longing for the other as we did that night.

That evening was a magical time that I still see clearly in my mind as I write this now. However, in time, it will be just another memory like other things that have happened over the years. But it will be a good memory, nonetheless, when it surfaces at some future time now unknown.

The Date in the Park

Our second date was unusual, I think. How many folks have a picnic on a table in a park with German food and beer on a hot summer day? Well, we did that the weekend after our first date.

I had gone to the German deli in Grapevine and got some sausage and cheese, and I bought some German beer at Hall's Market south of there. Hall's had a huge selection of imported beer, so I got some good German brew and put it on ice for the outing.

You once more came over to my house, and we saddled up and drove to Trinity Park. The day was pretty hot, and I was reminded of the infamous Mayfest storm that had plowed through there and destroyed the Mayfest event along with a billion dollars of damage to homes, cars, and businesses. Plus, it killed a few people. But no hail storm was forecast that day—just sun, fair weather clouds, and of course, high humidity, which put us in the shade on a picnic table by the truck.

We spread out the goodies and opened the cold beer, ate, and talked for a long time about a lot of stuff—even things in our lives that were very painful to us. But we were comfortable with each other that day, and we opened up a lot to each other on topics that were intimate, personal, and sometimes hard to talk about. I do not think most people are inclined to do that so soon with someone, but we did; and I think it increased our attraction to each other quite a bit. Not that we needed much encouragement then.

Notes to Stephanie: Days Remembered

Many people seem to think that when you go on a date, you have do something dramatic and spend a large amount of money to impress the other person. But we did not do that on that fine day. We just enjoyed the simple pleasures of some good food and fine beer, so the drama was in what we talked about and how it brought us closer together.

That was the play we acted out on the stage of life that day. It was a good thing to do. Not some contrived and overdone production that many are prone to do. There are many people in life, who do not seem to be able to appreciate doing something simple. That is their loss, since simple things are sometimes the seed from which something greater sprouts and grows. Just as our talk over lunch in the park was one of the seeds for our budding relationship on that hot and wonderful July day in the park.

Seeing Mama Mia

You took me out on a date—yes, you did. A lady asked a man out on a date. I thought it was nice and somewhat unique based on what I had experienced with most past girlfriends. And what you wanted to do was unique as well: see a specific musical at the Bass Hall, which I had never been in. And that musical, *Mama Mia*, was your favorite, which I learned was also very well-known.

Like most guys, I am not a fan of musicals; but I, of course, went with you since I appreciated the fact that you asked me out and not the other way around. So as the day approached, I wondered about just what *Mama Mia* was and why you liked it so much. And when the day came, I was pleasantly surprised and also enlightened.

I remember parking in the tall garage across the street from the Hall and walking into its grand and beautiful structure. People were dressed in a variety of ways—some more formal than others; but on the whole, everyone was dressed up to some degree. We went to our seats and sat down overlooking the grand sweep of the interior of the building and the several decks with boxes and seats in them. Then the curtain finally opened, and the performance began.

Recounting the story of that musical is not needed here; one can find that on many websites and such. But what I will tell here is that I actually enjoyed it. I had not seen such a production since I was a kid, and that was a long time ago. But I was impressed by the acting and enjoyed the music as well. All in all, it was a very interesting and satisfying thing to see—especially since I really never liked musicals. But I liked that one, I must admit.

After it was over, we went to your favorite sushi place on the far west side of town near where you used to live. You went into some detail as we drove there about how good the food was and how the chef was very good at what he did. That was true as I found out. The sushi was truly outstanding, especially the fried shrimp heads. Fried heads of aquatic creatures are not for everyone, but they were good for us that day.

They were crispy, flavorful, and cooked well by a friendly chef from Japan, who somehow found his way to Fort Worth where people are more comfortable with steak, Mexican food, and hamburgers. There is nothing wrong at all with those Texas and Cowtown staples—I love them like the next man. But we both like different things to eat than what is normally consumed.

Finally, we finished up our meal, and that was the end of our date that day. It was a fun time, filled with two things that were new to me. Seeing a musical and eating shrimp heads were different, but good nonetheless, and I liked new things.

While I like variety, I feel there are a lot of people who are unwilling to try something new. This is not to say one should try something dangerous or do something that has no appeal, but examining a couple of new things is part of the spice of life.

And that day was such a time for trying that tasty spice: such days were rare and fleeting. That day was one which I will not forget as time goes on and new things appear to be sampled and enjoyed like we did together that July day.

I Love You

After we decided we were an item and were "going steady" as people in our generation used to say, I was invited to the open house of the Texas and Pacific Building by a lady who was an acquaintance of mine. With you having your real estate license still and me once having had one, it was a natural event for us to go to.

The Texas and Pacific (T&P) building was redone and turned into condominiums, changing the space once used decades ago for offices by the T&P railroad into cozy lofts and spaces for the urban dwellers of modern life. Not my type of place to live, but I wanted to see it, and you were curious about how they had redone the whole building and the prices of the units.

Like on our other dates, we climbed into my old F150 and drove downtown and parked by the building on Lancaster Street. Lancaster itself was also being reborn after the demolition of the now infamous I-30 Overhead and the re-routing of I-30 south of the T&P. Rebirth and renewal were in the air and still are in downtown Fort Worth.

We went in the building and presented our invitation to gain access to the event. We walked around and talked to the lady who invited me to the gathering—her name I now forget. We partook of the drinks and Hors D'Oeuvres and looked around. As we got up to see the spaces and units, we ran into my city councilman, Danny Scarth, who we talked to briefly. Of course, I said I was one of his constituents, which was true since I voted for him.

Notes to Stephanie: Days Remembered

We went up and looked at more than one of the units, thinking they were all a bit small; but the models that were open were nice, and we thought they would sell. We exited one, and out of curiosity, went to the end of the hall where there was a little alcove. With no one around, we naturally embraced and kissed a little—your leg was wrapped around me, which was sexy indeed. You were a pretty sight in your black dress and black hose. We certainly liked each other and perhaps the drinks we had added some fuel to that fire. After that, we did not stay there long, but we soon left and drove through downtown, going north towards Weatherford Street or Belknap Street. And that is when it happened.

I do not specifically remember now what we were talking about exactly, but you said you loved me and caught yourself. I asked you back, "So do you really love me, Stephanie?"

You paused as we went past some building and you said yes, you did and looked at me. I, of course, replied back that I loved you as well. Our feelings were in sync, of course; I had no doubt about it. We had progressed beyond merely being a couple or just casually dating and were getting to the "serious" stage.

And thus our relationship changed and was born again, you might say. Just as the T&P and Lancaster Street were being redone and becoming something new, so were we. We also changed by saying those three little words—"I love you"—to each other in my old Ford pickup in downtown Fort Worth that very lovely summer evening now years ago.

Notes to Stephanie: Days Remembered

Eating Lunch Together

One of the favorite things we did together was to eat lunch when you were not teaching, and I still had to go to work. That was something outside of our normal routine—at least the routine during the school year.

On the days we dined, I was always excited to see you pull into the parking lot in the Camry and know you were there in the lobby for me. I so enjoyed seeing you pretty and dressed up for me on those days; you looked good, and I was proud of you. And, of course, it was fun to show you off to my coworkers.

But actually, dining with you was the true peak of that little mountain of pleasure. Most of the time, given where I worked then, we ate at the Cracker Barrel on I-35W and Meacham. In a small way, it was the center of our joint universe since it was not far from our home or from your old house. In many ways, we were both close to familiar places when we sat there and dined.

And dined we did. I always liked Cracker Barrel and its home-style southern food whether it was chicken and dumplings or chicken fried steak. I was always satisfied when we left there. Being diabetic, I had to turn down their deserts; but in my mind, that was nothing to be sad about since having you with me at lunch, instead of griping coworkers, was the real main course and treat.

Sometimes, I think of those cozy little lunches we had there. They were fine meals in more than one way; they featured a full and hearty menu of food, love, and companionship that we both ordered from. And from that rich buffet and cornucopia, we ate with gusto on those hot summer days when you were not in school. All the meals of life should be that way for two people in love. And if that is so, both their stomachs and souls will be nourished and full.

Jeffery W. Turner

In The Game Room Together

The game room upstairs is my favorite room in the house. Before I met you, it was simply my own room for my "toys." The shelves were full of the hundreds of books and games I had accumulated since I was a kid. The two 4x8 tables always had a game set up on them and some book related to it was spread out nearby. Pictures that I liked, especially the one with my relative flying his B-17 in 1943, adorned the walls. And finally the air-hockey table my mom and dad gave my sister and me when I was 15 was there along with the big leather chair from my dad's office in Fort Worth. I was surrounded with things that I liked and also by things that related to my family and the memories about them. It was indeed my kingdom in more than one way.

Notes to Stephanie: Days Remembered

And then you came along. I remember on our first date I showed you "The Sanctum" as I called it. I think you were a bit surprised by its contents. Strangely, you had seen a wargame before at a garage sale. Too bad we weren't going together then since it sounded like the old man selling his wargames had some games worth some money. If you had called me about it, I would have immediately gone to his house in Lake Country and scooped up the goodies to resell them. But that little fantasy was not to be. Something different would arise. The Sanctum would become our playroom—not just mine.

After we moved you in, we put away some of my stuff, and I ceded part of The Sanctum to you for your bead work. Before then, you had your hobby things on your dining table downstairs. I realized that I really didn't need both tables, and I could box up some of my books to make room for your hobby delights.

And that I did. Soon we were both up there; you stringing beads and me pushing cardboard counters over maps in my paper wars. For a long time, we did that on many days of the week after dinner and work. After we went walking or played disc golf, we exercised our minds in The Sanctum. What had in the past been just my "Holy Of Holies" was now your shrine for enjoyment as well.

And enjoy it we did—even making love on the floor by one of the tables one night when we were feeling somewhat frisky. Certainly, we did like being up there in more than one way. It was a good place to be where we could pursue our own interests and yet be together as a couple. That was a good thing. Many couples are so into doing things alone; they forget what it is like to be a couple.

Notes to Stephanie: Days Remembered

It seems a sad thing that every couple does not have a room or place to share things together, and at the same time, do things they alone savor and enjoy. If every couple had their own joint Sanctum, they could savor the best of those worlds, just as we did for awhile up there as two individuals.

Jeffery W. Turner

Our Wedding Day

Our wedding day was a very good day as such days usually are. It was a day with comfortable temperatures and a lot of sun. It was a fun and joyous day for the two of us. It was a simple, but meaningful affair, which we had planned together over the previous months since we decided to marry that day at the boat races by your house.

Indeed we did plan it together; it was not just some girl's affair. Being a project manager, I had a list of to-dos. You, being more creative, did things like write most of our wedding vows. It was truly a joint effort since we did not tell many people what we were doing. When the preparations were all done, the church reserved, and the reverend was at hand, we were ready to

Notes to Stephanie: Days Remembered

go to Fort Worth Unity Church with our kids and their significant others.

My kids arrived at my house; we got in my truck and drove over to the church, running a few minutes late due the traffic they drove through. As we went around Loop 820, I kept thinking about you and what you would look like that day. The short drive seemed very long since like most grooms, I was a bit anxious and yet excited, too. We drove into the parking lot, got out, and walked up to the building; and I remember seeing you get out of your truck with your beautiful wedding dress on. The simple cream colored dress fit you so well. Your hair was up and very pretty. Too bad you forgot the headband you had on when we had our wedding pictures taken. A minor snafu, for sure, but most affairs like these have some.

Next, we gathered in the chapel of the church, and got started. Our vows were short, and Reverend Roach, of course, added some of his good words to ours to fully create our ceremony. I vividly recall looking in each other's eyes and putting on our rings, finally saying "I do" and hearing the reverend pronounce us, "husband and wife." And so we were. It was done, and we were one.

After it was all done, I also remember you were upset at your daughter, who snickered at some of Reverend Roach's words during the ceremony. I have a picture of you with an irritated look on your face taken after we had talked about that. In short, all weddings are a combination of fun, bliss, and some irritation. It is the nature of things when a family gathers, you know. Ours was no different that day.

Keeping to our desire to keep things simple, we next had dinner downtown at Texas De Brazil with the kids and their dates. A fine meal was had, we took a few more pictures to add to what was done at the church, and everyone went home. We went to my house and had our wedding night, of course. We went to sleep and awoke the next day as an official married couple. And thus, our time together really began.

In the end, our little wedding was like so many others. It had meaning spoken in our vows, we had our loved ones near us and broke bread together as a family, and we loved on each other in our warm wedding bed. It was a wonderful and magical day, for sure. All days should be like that even though the reality of life tells us that cannot be so. But regardless of the difficult nature of existence, we should all hope for such things to come to pass and hope they are lasting and full.

The Battleship and the Bistro

On one of the trips to see Jane in Galveston, we did something that was just for me but later turned into something we all enjoyed. That was the day we saw the battleship USS Texas in La Porte and had lunch in Kima on the way back to Galveston. The battleship and the bistro, if you will.

Since my childhood, I always enjoyed ships—especially the ones from World War II. I had been to Pearl Harbor and seen the silent wreck of the USS Arizona oozing oil next to Ford Island. And I had also seen the USS Alabama in Mobile. But regardless of the histories of those more famous ships, my favorite was the USS Texas BB-35.

Since Galveston is close to the battleship, I insisted we go there. And that we did one morning with Jane and Jimmy. That day was sunny and humid; being near Houston, it would have been almost unnatural for it to be otherwise. We drove into town and went to where the ship was moored, which is near the San Jacinto battlefield.

We drove up to the ship, parked, got our tickets, and went aboard. As do most people, we went from deck to deck in the bowels of the ship and also upwards through parts of the superstructure of the nearly 100-year-old behemoth. We all enjoyed looking through the portholes and sitting on the seats of the old 40MM Bofors anti-aircraft guns. Being there was a window back into time and our military history. We took some pictures and decided to return to Galveston.

Notes to Stephanie: Days Remembered

We climbed into the truck and started driving back to I-45. During that part of the trek, we knew generally where we were but not exactly, and that is when the fun started. We were going south on some state highway, and it was lunch time; my blood sugar would need to be fed. So, we started looking for some place to stop. After we went over some overpass, our ultimate, but accidental, destination came into view. That was the Kima resort area filled with shops and restaurants. Needing lunch, we decided to stop there.

Kima was a place I had heard of but had never been to. It was on Galveston Bay and was filled with people that day. Couples with young kids, families like ours, and other examples of local humanity were walking through the sea of shops and dining establish-ments. We found something that appealed to all of us and went in for lunch.

The restaurant's name escapes me now, Razoo's maybe, but we had a very good time in there. We had some drinks, which were good on that warm day, and of course, devoured some seafood surrounded by other tourists and locals in the dining area ringed by windows overlooking all things Kima.

After eating, we went into some of the shops. While that was mostly for Jane, the rest of us also viewed the "human zoo" of people milling around the busy place and the stores. Maybe it was the effects of the drinks at lunch, but it was fun to be there with all of you; and coupled with seeing the battleship, it had turned out to be a great day.

But all good things must come to an end, as the old saying goes, and we climbed back into the truck and drove back to Galveston on I-45—

still seeing some signs of Hurricane Ike's destructive visit along the way. And we talked about where we would go for dinner that night as well. Landry's, wasn't it?

Thinking back, that day was a very good day—perhaps one of my favorites in a long time. We were surrounded by each other and also by things that gave us pleasure as individuals and also together as a family. There are not many better things than that in one's life. Thus, the battleship and the bistro were a good combination for us all on that bright, sunny day on the Gulf.

Jeffery W. Turner

Driving Around Lake Country

One of your favorite places to drive through was Lake Country Estates off of Boat Club Road. We went there many times and drove through its tree lined streets with fine homes built in decades past. A wonderful older neighborhood that you loved and one I learned to appreciate as well.

And why did we like it? For me, it was simply the look of the area. The style of the homes harkened back to an earlier more stable time; the fully grown trees told a story of a time when people were less mobile and were more prone to stay in one place. The gentle rolling hills, which sloped down to Eagle Mountain Lake and up to the rolling prairies above Lake Country, gave it a feel that few other places in that area have. The newer areas close to it did not have the same feeling—that is for sure. Indeed, it was something unique and a place where I would have been content to live.

But we never got the chance to live there for several reasons. It is still there, of course— an enclave locked in a stasis of sorts that harkens back to a *Leave It to Beaver* time. It is more surrounded than ever by the growing sea of newer, cookie-cutter tract homes that will someday wash up to its very shores and beyond, across the rolling prairies . But even so, its tranquility will remain for many years to come and will be home to families and people who hopefully will appreciate its stately and quiet grandeur as we did.

Jeffery W. Turner

Bonds Ranch Road: The View of Forever

Do you remember the day we drove around in the country and went on Bonds Ranch Road and parked on the top of the hill with the gorgeous view to the west? Remember the hill with the view that is both huge and beautiful, which seems to go on forever?

The expanse one sees was not infinite, however; but in earlier times, like the frontier era, it might as well have been infinite given the fact that people then seldom left their immediate area, never straying much from their farms, ranches, or towns. What one saw covered all of western Tarrant County and also parts of Parker and Wise as well. Looking southwest, one could also see the ridge of hills that overlooked parts of Hood and Johnson

Notes to Stephanie: Days Remembered

Counties beyond. The panorama was certainly grand in its sweep and the areas it covered.

This view of the countryside covered places we both had been to or had lived near at various times in our lives. In a way, the view there was a picture of our lives: the places were the results and mileposts of choices made in the past. From there, you could see where you were and perhaps see where you might go, depending on what you might choose within the bubble of your own individual universe of existence.

So, there we were one sunny Sunday in the truck or maybe it was the Camry with a six pack of Stella Artois, discussing the nature of the universe and our lives while looking across the rolling terrain towards Eagle Mountain Lake. That day was very nice with you; it really was. Bright sunshine, and the sunshine of what we had with each other, along with that pretty view made me feel alive and well with things overall.

It is still a nice and wonderful place even with the sea of houses starting to encroach upon its rolling prairies and grass-filled pastures from the east. I still go there sometimes to ponder things like the past, the present, and of course, the future and what it may hold. Except when a car drives by, the only thing heard is the sound of the wind blowing through the grass as it has for eons. And thus, the gentle noise of the breeze is the soundtrack to one's reflection under the sky, overarching the world. You are not with me now, but life goes on while the world around us remains.

With or without houses on its grounds, Bonds Ranch Road will always be a special place to me. It will always have a *View of Forever* on top of its hill, regardless of what is around me there.

Jeffery W. Turner

The Hill at Heritage

During our drives looking at houses and the country, I always liked places that had a view overlooking the country from some high vantage point. Bonds Ranch Road was my favorite place like that; but one day, we found a good spot not far from home. That place was the hill at Heritage.

In our area, the sea of houses spread into every possible piece of developable land. Pastures, farms, and fields were gobbled up and paved over with tract homes of various sizes and shapes. Such was the result of a growing city and was to be expected. But one place I thought would not be touched was the three hills that ran southeast to northwest in the southern part of Keller that was a couple of miles from my house.

Notes to Stephanie: Days Remembered

Those post and black jack oak-covered hills were the western edge of the eastern belt of the Cross Timbers. The Cross Timbers were definitely different from the prairies they abut to, which inspired a book about them called *The Cast Iron Forest*.

But describing the physiographic region and its characteristics is not the point of this note. Instead, it is the view from one of its hills that is the point.

Before I met you, I went walking on those hills. There were fine views from them all. On one you could see downtown Dallas; from the others, downtown Fort Worth was in plain view along with the rolling terrain to the west and places beyond like Bonds Ranch Road. At that time, you could not drive up to those points, but that changed as new homes were being built up to the sides of the hills.

Being curious about the layout of one of the new developments along Heritage Trace Parkway, we drove around the streets to find a pocket of land with streets nestled in the gap between two of the hills and sloped upward. We soon found the highest vantage point, which had a gorgeous view to the southwest. Except for the houses below, it was a quiet and peaceful place surrounded on three sides by the hills.

And so we sat there, admiring the view that warm day. There was no haze or dust, so we could see a long way across the prairie and the houses below us. It was that way until the houses began springing up there, too. Brick and veneer blocked the once grand view of the land,

and we went back no more. That once spacious view was only a memory in my mind.

Such things do happen in life, you know. Many good things are like us—they are not eternal. They appear for a brief time and then are gone— never to appear again except in our mind's eye or within the ethereal fog of our dreams late at night.

And thus, we should be ever thankful for such things in our lives. We should always enjoy them when they are present for the day of their absence will be at hand sooner than we might imagine or want. So when a beautiful view is there, take the time to look from it. Cast your eyes upon the magic that is before you. Be thankful for a view of the far horizon that is given to you by time, nature, or even God.

Jeffery W. Turner

Painting the Bathrooms and Kitchen

Each summer when you were out of school, you did things like take your continuing education classes and do projects you wanted to do. The biggest project you did was repainting the bathrooms and the kitchen with that "sponge paint" theme.

You never really liked the décor of my house, and you started this project to change that—in case we sold the house to buy one together.

When school was out that summer, we had finally ruled out new wallpaper and had decided to paint. I let you choose the colors. You bought paint and supplies, and you went to work by first scraping off the wallpaper everywhere. While I did help with that phase, you did the vast majority of the work. You went room by room, removing the wallpaper and then putting on the base coat and the tedious "sponge" effect with more than one color of paint.

This did take awhile to do; but in the end. The result was very nice, and I always liked how it looked. I still like how it looks. I can say that effort was one of your finest hours

Jeffery W. Turner

Moving You In and Rearranging the House

After living at both of our houses, we finally decided to live in my house and rent yours out. As a result, we had a lot of moving to do—move some of my stuff to storage, move some of yours to storage, and move your stuff into my house. The movers were hired, and we did just that.

Now the move itself was not that memorable.. What was interesting was how you rearranged the house, especially the downstairs, and how folks reacted to the new look of the same old house.

We added your sectional divan, dining room set, cabinets for your glass pieces, and your bedroom suite in the master bedroom. We hung some of your pictures and added your plants and greenery to the rooms. All in all, you changed the way the place looked.

This type of change happened in many similar situations, but the "Kodak moment" of it all was when our neighbor Josh came over to help hoist my TV on top of your chest. The look on his face as he viewed how you transformed the house was priceless. Even though I had tasteful décor in the house before I knew you, his simple comment about the household mutations said it all: "Looks like a women lives here now." Indeed so. Josh had eloquently summed up what you had done to the house. Indeed, a woman now lived there, and it was a good thing to behold.

Renewing Our Vows at Unity Church

After getting married, you wanted to renew our wedding vows each year on our anniversary. At first, I thought the idea was kind of silly, but I came around and thought it would be good just as you did.

The question then was what exactly would we do when we did that? You and I talked about it; and you wanted the good Reverend Roach, who married us, to administer the same vows, slightly changed perhaps, at the church. The next question was where at the church would he perform the service for us? That answer came to us, too. We decided to do the vows in the gardens around the church school and office as opposed to in the chapel where we had wed—specifically in the area called The Labyrinth, which is the gravel and stone garden under the big oak tree on the north side of the church school. Finally, we set the date and time for our first renewal and went there that day. We waited for the Reverend underneath the tree, looking at the stones arrayed beneath it.

We walked in the paths of The Labyrinth, thinking about what it symbolized. We strolled through its concentric circles of stones under the big oak tree and wondered aloud what it meant. When the Reverend arrived, we quickly got down to the business at hand. We held hands, followed his lead, and repeated the words that had been spoken before to join us together. But they were said now to reaffirm that pledge made one year before. When we were through with vows, we took some pictures.

As we did after our wedding, we thanked the good Reverend Roach, told him goodbye, and went out for dinner. We left the church and dined at Texas De Brazil. Just as before, the food was wonderful along with the drinks. Finally, we left and drove home, got romantic, and fell asleep to end a wonderful day.

We repeated that ceremony one more time after that night, going to the church and then going out to dinner like we had done on our wedding day. The words of our vows were a creation of us as a couple, and we repeated them as such.

But now with us apart, the words of our vows were for not. Perhaps when we were fussing, we should have both remembered the fine words we had crafted together in the exciting time before our wedding; and more importantly, the three times we said them to each other with the good and kind Reverend Roach at our side. If we had done that, perhaps we would have had more times in The Labyrinth to remember together and not just the solitary memories we have now.

Wedding Picture Day

Cathy Zaragoza was the wife of my former drinking buddy Steven "Estevan" Zaragoza, whom I had met when I had some beers up at Up In Smoke BBQ in Keller. Former drinking buddy since we later learned that he had suddenly died. That was a shock and a surprise —Steven was always a friendly guy and nice to everyone. Thus, I was glad we chose Cathy, who was a professional photographer, to do our wedding pictures.

We contacted her and set the date for the pictures as we had set the date of our wedding on the upcoming Halloween. You went out with your daughter and bought your wedding dress to prepare for the pictures.

Notes to Stephanie: Days Remembered

Well, they weren't really wedding pictures but pre-wedding portraits, you might say, since we did them in her studio at her house before we were married. But that was okay as we weren't doing our wedding in a totally traditional way.

We drove over to her house, you had your dress with you, and I had my best suit. I remember us both changing into our wedding attire. I was certainly pleased to see you in your cream-colored dress with your hair all fixed up. You looked very pretty indeed: no woman was more beautiful than you were that fine fall day.

So, Cathy took a series of shots of us together and each of us alone that day. They turned out very well, and we ordered a set of them for our wedding album. After we wed, I had some of the pictures of you on my desk at work and at home. They showed a beautiful woman smiling big at the world. People always remarked on how pretty you were.

Those pictures were very nice of us. They showed how happy we were then and how anxious we were to wed. They were a record of something wonderful we had in the past that is now gone. Regardless of the state of things with us now, the pictures will never change, even though in the end we did.

Notes to Stephanie: Days Remembered

Zestfest with Mom

Ahhh...Zestfest—the king of hot sauce shows, which graces Fort Worth in the late summer as the heat outside begins to wane and the glories of fall are all around. But the heat does not go away inside of the show. Instead, the show provides a wide array of products that will fill you with heat, and sometimes agony, if you eat something that is too hot for you.

And going there had other effects as well. The idea for using a private label hot sauce for our wedding announcement was born at ZestFest by the Old Gringo Chile Company, which was an exhibitor when we were engaged.

Since we both liked hot foods and my extended family liked such things too, we made plans to attend it together with some of them on a

Saturday in August. When the day arrived, we drove down to Will Rogers where it was held and met Mom at the front door. We bought our tickets and cruised through the aisles of booths, tasting new sauces and other hot and spicy products. As usual, many things we tried were bad but a few were really good. We, of course, bought a few things here and there to add to our already large stock of hot sauces. With the heat of the products on our tongues, we got more than one cold beer to wipe away the incendiary fluids tormenting our mouths. But the torment was a good form of pain. That was the point of trying hot stuff.

While we tried a lot of new things, the highlight of the day was not sampling everything but watching you in the jalapeño eating contest. While you loved hot foods like me, I never imagined you would try that. There was some big door prize like a widescreen TV, and that made you want to do it.

They filled everyone's bowls with a large pile of very big and juicy peppers, and then the contest began. Watching the victims...I mean contestants... it was clear you would not win. There were folks in the line with you who had done this before. They usually swallowed the peppers whole—almost without chewing. But you gave it your best and consumed a bunch of the peppers. I loved hot stuff as much as you did, but I was not willing to risk the wholesale public destruction of my stomach and intestines for a prize that day.

I do not remember if you had digestive track upheaval later that day or if a pyroclastic flow of sorts erupted from your bowels in some violent intestinal super eruption but I know you had fun trying to best your pepper consuming rivals that day at Will Rogers Coliseum. We of course had to get you a cold beer to clean some of the capsaicin from your burning mouth.

After that experience, things were a bit anticlimactic. We walked around some more and then left for home. My mom went back to Granbury, and we went back to north Fort Worth, satisfied that we had went.

Zestfest was always fun to attend. Certainly on that Saturday, one could say it was a hot night (actually day) out on the town. A hot and satisfying time in the oven of Zestfest was had by all, and we survived to eat more hot stuff another day.

Tommy's Hamburgers

A good hamburger is hard to find they say. Tommy's Hamburgers was always good and easy to find. Tommy's was a service station/hamburger stand chain in the area. One of its locations was on northwest Loop 820 in Lake Worth at Navajo Trail. When we started dating and going together, we went there since it was near your house. But the reason for going there was not just the location, it was because the burgers were always delicious and fresh.

Not to mention the fact that since it was also a convenience store, so one could help one's self to a cold six pack of beer to consume with the burger, fries, and onion rings. It was one of those places you might see on *Diners, Drive-ins, and Dives*— a roadhouse, if you will. No matter what you called it, they had very good food; and it was popular with the locals.

The way they prepared their fare was classic local grub. The patty was thin and grilled on a flat metal grill. The buns were toasted and then mated with the meat, cheese, lettuce, tomatoes, onions, pickles, and either mayo, mustard, or both. And, of course, since it's in Texas, you could get a bunch of jalapeños added. The rings and fries were hot and crispy, just waiting for a good squirt of ketchup to fix them up as well. The fare was truly excellent and filling food that was nothing fancy but always delicious and fresh.

We ate there on several occasions when we were working on your house or just for lunch or supper when we felt like it or were over on that side of town. And we weren't the only people there; on any day, there were always an assortment of cars parked on the side of the building or getting gas.

Another thing about Tommy's was the fact that since you had eaten there for years and the people behind the counter had been there that long also, we always had friendly service. Going there was more than just getting a fresh, hot burger, it also made you feel good and made you feel like you were around friends. Truly Tommy's was special and not some cookie-cutter hamburger chain like McDonald's with its mediocre, tasteless, and faceless fare.

So when the Lake Worth Tommy's service station was sold to Navajo (there are other surviving Tommy's Hamburgers stores; the Lake Worth 820 location was the original Tommy's, by the way), it was a very sad day indeed since we heard the hamburgers were no more.

If the Lake Worth Tommy's had been a person, its funeral would have had many mourners present. We probably would have been amongst that sad throng, hoping it would somehow be resurrected to live again and to cook more fine meals for its faithful disciples—not just be a little footnote in the area's culinary history that in a few years, no one would remember.

But in fact they still make hamburgers there. It is now called Navajo Burgers. So in a way, the Lake Worth Tommy's continues: the folks on the grill there will tell you, "We make the same hamburgers; we just have a different name." That small name change does teach us that nothing lasts forever. We all get used to favorite places we frequent; but like many things, they change into something else.

So the burgers do live on and are just as good as they used to be. (I had the cheddar jalapeño burger recently.) It's the same thing; it's just different as the old saying goes. The same grill and meat are there; it's just called something different. And thankfully for the pallets of its many loyal patrons, the report of that hamburger joint's demise was premature and exaggerated indeed.

Jeffery W. Turner

Roof Repairs and Such

One of the most interesting things we ever did was repair both of our roofs after the big windstorm the first year we were married. That particular storm happened early in the storm season and did some relatively minor damage to both of our roofs. Not needing a roofer, we foxed the damage ourselves.

The funny thing about this chore was that you, the very feminine lady that you are, were more eager to climb up on the roof than I was. You did, and we were both up there replacing shingles those two sunny days, so we would not incur the expense for someone to fix something thing that was easy for us to do.

I clearly remember us on your house, for example, nailing the shingles in and also enjoying the view from up on the top of your two story house. Arrayed around us was your neighborhood, and we could also see much more of the lake and surrounding area than we could at ground level. Being up there naturally gave us a different point of view of our surroundings. It was not quite God-like, but we were on top of our little part of the world. And we had the same perspective on top of my house as well. A small change in viewpoint can show someone a lot.

And perhaps that is the point of describing the views seen on those days. Many people seem to be unaware of what can be seen in their own neighborhoods and surroundings. If you drive around and stop some place where you have not been before, new vistas are unveiled if you simply pause to look around. Sometimes a small change in place or vantage point can open up many new things to explore and enjoy.

Many people these days are too busy to stop their harried pace and do that. But we did stop, which was one more advantage we had nailing shingles those days instead of paying a roofer.

Notes to Stephanie: Days Remembered

Winter Storm Damage

In late winter of 2007/2008, we had a little winter surprise at your house, which we were then renting out. That surprise was the sudden and unexpected heavy snow fall that spread across our part of Tarrant County one day.

There were several inches of the white stuff on the ground; and as usual, any amount of snow was the end of the world it seemed. Traffic was crawling or snarled all around our area.

That, in and of itself, was not that big of a deal since contrary to popular belief it does snow in our part of Texas—sometimes a lot in one storm. The real issue for us was the phone call from the renters. They called with the shocking news that your metal patio awning had collapsed and was destroyed by the snow and ice. The weight of the frozen mass was too much for the metal sheets and posts. It could not endure the weight any longer and fell to the patio below.

We both went over there after work with the camera, and the sight was something I had never seen before in a snowstorm. After thunderstorms, there was always damage like we saw that day—but not after our area had been turned into a "winter wonderland." There, in front of us, was twisted sheet metal, crumpled metal posts, and parts of the siding all heaped together in a tangled mass covering your patio.

This disaster meant something to you; it was more than just irritation from the damage itself. It was more important to you than normal since you had built the awning by yourself with some help from your kids. You had described to me how you built it with supplies and tolls from the Home Depot up the road in Lake Worth. But now it was a pile of junk for a metal scrap yard on the north side of town. Your great work, done with care and skill, was now just refuse on the ground, and the task then was to replace what had been destroyed. So over the next few weeks, we filed the insurance claim, removed the wreckage, and had someone rebuild it since we were short on time—the renters needed it rebuilt since the back door was blocked by the pile of debris.

Certainly, this episode shows that the old saying about Texas weather changing all of the time is true, but it also shows that you never know what a person is capable of doing simply by how he or she looks. Not too many attractive ladies with a doctorate could have built a metal patio awning, thirty feet long, mostly on their own. But you did build that awning, and that is the real story here to be told. Just because a pretty girl wears a dress, it doesn't keep her from swinging a hammer or a wrench.

Notes to Stephanie: Days Remembered

Smoking A Turkey With Your Son

On many a Thanksgiving and Christmas, my dad would fire up his smoker and cook a turkey and a ham in it. He would build the fire near bedtime, let it burn down, and then put the meat on and let it cook all night until it was done. When we woke up in the morning, we would test the meat for doneness, and when ready, take it off of the fire and carve it up. We savored the freshly roasted meat and the cracklings as delicacies. It certainly was good food, and so I kept doing the same thing as do other members of the family.

But the part of that experience I liked the best, especially as an adult, was not just eating the meat, but standing by the smoker in the dark and the cold and having a drink with my dad and shooting the breeze. We would have a beer or a Jack Daniels, and the smoke wafted around us while the cold wind blew, too. Maybe the moon was out, or maybe it was just a dark, starry night; but it was a special time we had on those holidays at my mom and dad's that always meant a lot to me. So when we married, I wanted to show your son the same thing since he had no dad to show him such things, and I wanted him to have the same warm memories of holiday times as I did.

And I did just what my dad did. I got out the charcoal, soaked the mesquite chips, and set the thing ablaze, showing him how I did it. I also told him how much fun I had with my dad, smoking a turkey when he was alive. So, we got the fire burning and had some drinks in the dark like me and my dad had on the last Thanksgiving we were together.

Notes to Stephanie: Days Remembered

In comparison to showing your son how to smoke meat, hearing how you could not roast a turkey was funny indeed. You and he both recounted how you simply stuck a frozen bird in the oven one Thanksgiving and were given back a half-cooked, inedible bird. Thus, when you and your kids had smoked turkey and ham, you were indeed having something new and delicious.

However, moving beyond how to smoke meat and how not to roast a turkey, the times spent by a fire are special times between a father and son. It really isn't a motherly thing to stand by a fire and drink booze, you know. I always will remember the times spent in the swirling mesquite smoke with my dad. These simple events built solid memories of growing up and being together.

And most of all, I hope your son learned something from my instruction on how to smoke a big bird; and one year hence, he shows his son, or maybe a daughter, the same thing under a cold, starry sky. And may his turkey and ham be well done and enjoyed by all on that holiday yet to come.

Notes to Stephanie: Days Remembered

Your Students Love You

One thing that always amazed me was how well you did with the little kids who were your students. Each time I saw you with one of them, it was obvious they respected and loved you. The way one of them would reach up and give you a hug was one way your skill as a teacher showed itself to the world.

Each time I went to one of your school functions, I saw that happen. If the kids were not hugging you, one of the parents expressed their thanks to you. It was a shame that school protocol would not let you hug the kids back. For many of your kids, such a display of caring or love from you might be the only loving gesture they would see that day. Their home environments lacked parents who gave them that common kindness and love. That is something many of us take for granted but is more common in society than we can imagine. The fact that you did more than merely teach in your classes showed how much you really cared about your students.

Many times, you would tell me about one kid who had made special progress or had a nice, little personality that got your attention. Such kids made you smile, but you cared for the ones who had a hard time just as much. More than once, you spent extra time with a pupil who needed help or discipline to finish his assigned lessons. You kept trying to help your students until they succeeded. The combination of care and skill as a teacher you had made a great difference with many children at your school. This success made you a master teacher indeed.

If you did anything wrong, it was that you did not know your limits sometimes. No matter how hard you tried, you could never help all of the kids to the extent they might have needed.

But that is nothing to criticize you about. It simply showed once more how much you loved all of the little kids you taught. And that was why they loved you.

Love given and love returned was the simple lesson you taught in your little classroom, which was really a big closet by the stage. That small, but profound, example not found in any textbook was hopefully the most important and lasting thing your students learned from you in their lives. Maybe one day they, like you, would care enough about some kid to simply give one a little hug.

Family Marriage Angst

When we started talking about marriage, we talked about the type of wedding we would have. Having both been married before, we did not want some huge affair and decided on something small.

Over time, we talked about whom we would invite. We discussed the options from simply having a justice of the peace marry us with no one present to inviting my extended family and your foster parents. In the end, we chose to have our kids present and to not tell anyone about it until after it was done. And that decision was our mistake.

We decided to mail out a wedding announcement to our families and friends, containing an invitation to a wedding party and our "secret" private label hot sauce we ordered from Old Gringo Chile Company. On our wedding day, I mailed them off; and we all gathered at the Unity Church and got married. Afterwards, we were off to dinner with the kids, and we thought all would be well. Boy, were we wrong on that assumption.

I remember the call from my sister, explaining how hurt and angry they were that we did not tell them in advance of our plans and the after-the-fact announcement. Your foster parents were miffed, too, but not as much as my family was. So, we sat in the den in a state of mutual shock over this and simply sat without words for a bit. We thought since we were not exactly fifteen years old, we did not have to announce it to everyone. In retrospect, we should have done that.

In the end, things were straightened out; and peace was restored in the family, but that situation, which was our first crisis as a married couple, showed that families have their own dynamics and do not behave like they are "supposed to" as is described in psychology textbooks or on some TV talk show.

People in a family have emotions; and since these emotions are about other family members, they are more intense than others.

Those feelings were something I should have realized would be present, but I did not; and we paid for that mistake with hard feelings that were not meant to be. Thus, the lesson of these events was that even when people did something out of the love they had for each other, they still needed to consider the viewpoints and feeling of others.

Notes to Stephanie: Days Remembered

What is innocent in one's own mind and done without a hurtful motive might not be seen that way by other people that are kin. The ties of family blood remain forever thicker than water. This was something we were reminded of in a painful way.

Jeffery W. Turner

Living at Two Houses

When we first got married, we had not decided where we would live—my house or yours. So for awhile, we lived in two houses at the same time. As opposed to someone with no place to live, we had two. And that is the story I would now like to tell.

We spent time at each other's houses before we wed, but we also kept doing that after we got married. I suspect that is something people do these days to one degree or another; but after a point, it does cause some logistical problems as a couple. But before that realization was made, it was fun to live in two places at once.

While I was travelling for business, I really started to dislike the process: pack, go, unpack, go some more, pack, go, and unpack in a

Notes to Stephanie: Days Remembered

seemingly endless torment of movement to here or there. But in our case, it was almost like what people, who had never done business travel might think: it would be fun. . Yes, it was fun to come home, grab my clothes, check the mail, get my insulin together, and then zoom down I-35W and Loop 820 to your house on the northwest side of town near Lake Worth. More than one once, I remember seeing the college campus and the Lake Worth water tower, and I knew I was about to land. I would exit off 820, drive into your neighborhood, and pull up to your house. We would hug and kiss, cook dinner, go walking, go to bed, and get up in the morning to go to work. And repeat that cycle the next day.

Then, the process would repeat itself, but in reverse, a day or two later. You would pack, get your stuff together, and then go down Loop 820 and up I-35W to my neck of the woods.

And so it went on for some time until we realized this was not practical—we had to have a home together. But regardless of that realization and the moving we later did, it was a fun, little time doing some "business travel" within our own town. The business in question was not of some commercial endeavor, but instead, it was the business of being a husband and wife who had just wed.

Notes to Stephanie: Days Remembered

Talking to Mom to Straighten Things Out

When the "you know what" hit the fan when we didn't tell our families before we got married, we were shocked. We both recoiled from the hurt and anger that my mom especially felt. Given the close nature of my family in the past, this turmoil could not continue.

Since you were an orphan, who never had any family outside of foster parents, you were also confounded by this. Regardless, this state of angst made for a rotten first holiday season with the clan.

The tension remained, and my kids were caught in the middle. Your kids had never met my family, except once before, so they were not really harmed by it all. When my mom wanted to talk to us about it, we dreaded the conversation, but we knew we needed to clear the air.

So one Sunday, we drove to Granbury to see her. We got to her place and sat down with her. No one else was there. We talked for some time, and she explained her hurt and anger towards what we had done. We could understand what she was saying, even though we both still felt we did not have to tell everyone in advance. She also said we should have told them after the wedding in person or on the phone, and not just send something in the mail. I could agree with that, and thus, we settled the matter and things returned to normal.

My mom never held a grudge against us, as you know. She always treated you well and also enjoyed and loved you, too. She always asked how you were doing and always welcomed us both to her place. Thus, the hatchet had indeed been buried, and life went on.

What was clear about this situation was sometimes a good thing could sprout from something that seemed to have nothing positive in it. The angst and anger that was felt gave way finally to love and welcome. All was forgiven and all bad feelings were put aside in favor of the previously peaceful state. That was something we should all remember.

Forgiveness is one way to happiness, and holding grudges and forgetting the feelings of others is the road to the opposite.

Jeffery W. Turner

When You Watched Me Mow

One day sometime before we got married, I needed to mow my yard. It was your turn to come over to my house for dinner and to spend the night. You were running late, and I was a bit miffed, even though I got over that and kept mowing to get it done before you arrived.

So, off I went pushing my Wal-Mart special mower over the grass and drinking some cold beer along the way that hot day in September.
I was in the backyard mowing the part west of the pool when you arrived. But I was so into the task at hand, I did not realize you were there. While I zigzagged across my backyard, you were standing in the open gate watching me in silence—something I did not notice for awhile. You later said you had stood there for awhile, maybe a couple of minutes at least, until I

finally noticed you there. Funny how that works sometimes, eh? You can be so engrossed in a chore or task that you do not see the one who loves you standing in plain view in broad daylight. But I did just that.

But not noticing you really is not the point I am trying to make. The point is that one can watch in silence something or someone loved in quiet reflection. That is, love for someone, or the appreciation of something, does not have to always be a public affair. It can be done from afar and in the silence of one's own mind. And in such a quiet time, the greatest enjoyment and admiration for that person or thing can sometimes be found.

Jeffery W. Turner

Talking About Marriage

In the movies, we see a man proposing marriage to his love in some dramatic setting like a fancy restaurant or in the natural grandeur of some majestic outdoor place. Instead of that type of almost mythical scene, we talked about getting married while sitting on some rocks at Marine Creek Lake, watching the boat races and drinking some Coors Light in the hot summer heat of Texas one August day.

Yes, leave it to us to do something in a way that no one else had ever done it. Now the setting in which we decided to get married made the decision no less important than a wedding decision made in a more traditional place. It was simply how we made the decision that was kind of funny and not so dramatic.

Notes to Stephanie: Days Remembered

As I said, we were sitting on some rocks out in the sun, watching the annual boat races. It was quiet after some of the loud race boats had zoomed by, but then it was really silent—except for a little wind, the waves lapping up on the rocks, and the sound of people talking in the distance. A few birds circled overhead, too, occasionally chirping something out to each other. It was a fine day to be outside.

We started talking about something. Exactly what escapes me now, but I said something in reference to couples breaking up. You replied, "What if we don't ever break up?"

I paused for a brief second, taking a swig of beer and said something back like we weren't going to break up. Bingo. And that was that. We talked some more and decided somewhat by accident to get married that day in August

2006 by a tree you could see from Loop 820 that peeked over the top of the dam.

So, you never knew what you might get at a boat race. Some got a prize for winning a race, others just walked around and drank oceans of cold beer in the sun. And a few others, like us, got engaged to be married.

Notes to Stephanie: Days Remembered

Shopping at Saigon Taipei Market

One of the favorite things that we started doing was shopping at the Saigon Taipei Market on Belknap Street at the border of Haltom City and Fort Worth. In that area populated by Asian immigrants, we found the usual "pho" shops and several oriental groceries and markets.

Many native Texans did not like going into those markets since they sometimes smelled funny to Americans, and many of the food items were simply unknown and unfamiliar to them. Also, the language barrier sometimes was another deterrent to "Bubba" shopping there.

Not so at Saigon Taipei. That store had nice wide aisles, signs in English, and people that spoke English; it also had the neutral smell of a typical American grocery store. Of course, there were a million food items you had no idea about, but one could find out about them from the staff. Since we had seen it driving by, we decided to shop there.

And thus, we went in there one Saturday afternoon on a sunny day to fill our car with many delectable goodies of all types. That day we bought fresh fish, the so-called "soo-goo," whose real name we did not know. But when we baked it, the soo-goo was a very tasty fish. We also bought fresh shrimp that I cooked on the smoker during the so-called "BBQ Shrimp Deluge," when we ate smoked shrimp two days in a row. And of course, I got some fixings for a stir-fry, consisting of two kinds of Bok Choy, fresh snow peas, and other fresh veggies that they had in profusion. On other visits, we bought clams for chowder, beef and pork tongue, which I cooked in green chile, frozen oriental dumplings of more than one type, and whole ducks, which I smoked. Yes, Daffy was indeed smoked and eaten whole to our mutual delight. And on top of the good taste of all of the ingredients, they were all very cheap when compared to similar items at a grocery store.

Saigon Taipei, therefore, was always a fun place to shop since I liked to cook and enjoyed trying new foods. Trying new things was a very good thing and literally added spice to our lives. That market, now out of business and closed unfortunately, was a large and satisfying helping of such seasonings that nourished our bodies and souls. Its full and varied aisles provided many new dishes to try on life's big buffet. A tasty treat it was indeed.

Jeffery W. Turner

Eating Daffy, Menudo, Tongue, and Grasshoppers, Too

After each trip to the grocery store of any type, especially the aforementioned Saigon Taipei, I always cooked up something new. Eating new foods, especially something that most people might recoil in horror from or turn their nose up at, was something I relished as much as the star of *Bizarre Foods* seemed to. While we never ate many of the things he did on his show, we certainly spread our culinary wings quite a bit over time. So this little note is a tale of some of our memorable *Bizarre Foods* recipes.

To begin, we examine The Cooking of Daffy the Duck. We bought a whole duck for the first time at our beloved Saigon Taipei market. The duck was whole, simply plucked with the head and feet still on the bird. Cooking him was simple. I spiced him up like I would a smoked chicken and put him on the smoker for three hours. He was crispy and done when he was removed from the coals. When we dined on Daffy's namesake and relative, the meat was good indeed. Tender, smoky, and delicious. Now it was not Peking duck mind you, but that Fort Worth duck was still good and something we did again.

Menudo is something that most gringos do not like, but something we both liked a lot. I made it several times using a modified recipe a Hispanic co-worker gave to me. It is simple to make, consisting of beef tripe, pigs' feet, onion, spices, water, and white hominy. All simmered for a few hours and served with tortillas, chopped onions, hot peppers, the ubiquitous squeeze of lime juice, and maybe a cold beer. Another worthy meal even though you still thought the menudo at Dos Molinas was better than mine. Perhaps so, but mine was still pretty good.

Now to lengua, which is beef or pork tongue. For some reason, people are really grossed out by the thought of eating tongue. But their nausea is not justified since those cuts of meat are very tender and do not have a weird taste at all. Cooked slowly in a sauce of fresh green chile peppers, they are a bit of heaven found in a bit of meat that one can serve up on a hot, fresh tortilla or even with some rice. Lengua is ann overlooked treasure chest in the sands of the food world.

After the above successes, we now turn to the one huge failure in this culinary tale: fried grasshoppers. Turning again to *Bizarre Foods*, we saw Andrew Zimmern eating bugs on more than one show. On one, he ate fried

Notes to Stephanie: Days Remembered

grasshoppers. We thought that maybe it would not be bad to try some. So lo and behold, one day at Saigon Taipei I found frozen grasshoppers in the frozen foods section. Yes, there were bags of these familiar bugs packed in Thailand and shipped here to be eaten. There were also cockroaches in the freezer: big, black, two-inch long insects in bags. That possible menu choice was far beyond even my ability to try, however.

But not so with the grasshoppers. We took our six-legged friends home, and I thawed them out and readied the wok for stir-frying. The oil got hot and in they went where I "chowed" them with some hot chili paste until they seemed to be crisp. I put them in bowls over fresh white rice, and the horror began. Chewing them up was not bad since they were crunchy—just like a potato chip or Cheetos. The problem was the taste: they tasted like the juice you get from chewing tobacco. That made me almost barf since it reminded me of the only time I tried "chaw" when I was 15 and had a major digestive eruption to the laughter of my dad. That was too much, and I disposed of mine and tried not to throw up. Few things nauseate me, but those bugs were something that did.

Well, three out of four bizarre things successfully tried wasn't bad, right? Probably so, and trying all of those things to eat was a lot of fun. So in my middle age now and having graduated past deli food, Hamburger Helper, Raman noodles, and fast food's horrors, I think life should be filled with such a buffet of new things from time to time since it adds pleasure and knowledge to life's meal. And they really do taste good most of the time. They really do!

Napping at the Symphony

Going to the Bass Hall in downtown Fort Worth is something one does with an amount of decorum since it is not some place for a happy hour or a noisy sports bar filled with drunks. Instead, people who enjoy the arts gather for the quite enjoyment of the symphony or a play.

We had done that before, going there with the "upper crust" to watch musicals and the like. We wore something other than a t-shirt with some beer brand on it, sat in our seats, and applauded when it was considered polite to do so. It was something you enjoyed and a thing I had learned to sometimes like, too.

And so I bought tickets for you to see the symphony, and we went there. But while there, I committed an unforgiveable sin in the eyes of the set that frequented the place.

The performance was on a Saturday afternoon. I ate lunch, but I also had a few drinks before we left. I had hoped the booze would enable me to endure the music better. Not liking symphonic music, I knew I would be bored stiff. Thus, I consumed some vodka and tonics to take the edge off of the upcoming acoustic torture. After lunch, we got dressed and drove downtown to the Great Hall.

We took our seats and the lights dimmed low. The music began, which to me was worse than someone running their fingernails down a blackboard or some tom cat howling and screeching at midnight. But I said nothing since

Notes to Stephanie: Days Remembered

the show was for you, and I listened with great discomfort.

The darkness, however, was my undoing. I started to feel sleepy, and then off I dozed. But that was not my real crime against the arts; my snoring was the abomination, especially to the elderly lady next to you, whom you said gave me a dirty look. That was in contrast to the young couple behind us, who laughed at the whole shameful affair.

I awoke, nonetheless, refreshed and was able to withstand more of the music. Thankfully, the performance ended, and we were able to leave the beautiful and truly grand Bass Performance Hall to go have some drinks—a dirty martini at the nearby 8.0 Bar. Regardless of what the orchestra was playing, my nap and snoring were the real performance that was noticed with chagrin by some art lovers that day. I trust the loyal patrons around us enjoyed my spontaneous nasal, narcoleptic recital and would remember it with great fondness each day. I know I will.

Notes to Stephanie: Days Remembered

Seeing Wicked at Fair Park

Another musical we saw was *Wicked*, which is a reinterpretation of *The Wizard of Oz* done with modern music. We went to see it on your birthday one year after our wedding at Fair Park Music Hall in Dallas. This show would not be playing at the Bass Hall in Fort Worth, so like Dallas's long time nemesis, Amon G. Carter, we bought tickets and reluctantly drove over there one Saturday.

The Fair Park Music Hall had been there for decades unlike the Bass Hall, but the atmosphere was similar and filled with the same type of people who enjoyed such things. I was, of course, dreading the whole affair since I hated musicals most of the time. (Seeing *Mama Mia* had softened my dislike and my negative opinion of musicals, however.)

But after the Hall darkened and the music began, I was pleasantly surprised by the musical score performed. It was theatre music, but it had chords and other artsy pop music features that I actually liked. I liked it so much I even got the CD of the soundtrack—the first time I had ever bought such a thing in my entire life.

In short, the whole thing impressed me, and I was surprised I liked it. And best of all, I did not fall asleep during the show like I did at the symphony orchestra performance at Bass Hall. This was fortunate for the people around us, and in the end, good for me since I got to hear all of the music, which changed my view of musicals forever. So, try a musical sometime; you might be surprised by what you hear.

Notes to Stephanie: Days Remembered

CERT Class: Starting to be Partners

We met by accident in Community Emergency Response Team class. We both wanted to serve the community, and we signed up for it not knowing the other and certainly not looking for a girlfriend/boyfriend there either. But that is what we got out of the class in the end. And how that happened was kind of funny.

We both remembered seeing the other the first time and thinking the other was cute. With this newfound and unexpected attraction, we started talking to each other, and I thought there was some mutual interest. But when you stopped talking to me, I was surprised. I was not aware until later that some of your erstwhile "friends" in Code Blue were giving you a hard time about it—something they kept doing even as our wedding approached. But that idiocy is not the story here; the story is how we resumed things.

One night in class, the topic was fire suppression. We would use fire extinguishers to put out a small fire in teams of two. The class teacher, Officer Lambert, along with a fireman explained how the drill would be done. Each team would have two members. One person would carry the fire extinguisher and the other, called a "buddy", would hold on to the first person, in case that person had to be pulled out to safety. After that simple explanation, you dropped the bombshell.

We were standing around talking as people were starting to pick partners, and you said something like, "We should become partners." Of course, you meant something besides just being partners in the class. So, we teamed up for the drill. I was in front first, with you holding on to me, and then we switched places. You later said that was fun and that it really turned you on to be able to hold on to my backside. The same was true for me. I liked your nice, curvy rear end, too.

I got the hint and asked for your phone number after class in the Police Academy parking lot, which led to our first date. And the rest, as they say, was history.

Jeffery W. Turner

Unity Church and Reverend Roach

Fort Worth Unity Church was the place where we married but also the place where we went to Church. You were a member there when we met, and I decided to attend with you since I liked what you told me about it.

Neither one of us was very religious by most standards, but I always enjoyed going there as opposed to what I usually felt when attending church. There were two reasons why I liked it. The first was the fact that they were not strict on their dogma or beliefs: you could believe what you wanted to. But the second was the most important—namely the good Reverend Paul John Roach and his messages.

Notes to Stephanie: Days Remembered

Certainly Reverend Roach, the man who married us, could be an example of the typical Unity member. He was smart, compassionate, and friendly. While an animated public speaker, he was soft spoken and always positive. When did he not smile? His sermons were always a pleasure to hear and were always filled with something that made us think about life. He never scolded and never preached hellfire and brimstone like so many preachers did. Instead, all he preached about was being good to thy neighbor and following the Golden Rule. All that he was could be summed up by those two simple, but profound, ideas that are found in many of the world's religions.

As much as we liked the place and the man, we should have gone more often, but we did not for a variety of reasons like being simply too lazy to get up and get going. But such is life; and in the end, it was our loss for missing out on many of his messages, which always filled our hearts and minds with so much good.

It goes to show that one should never miss out on a good thing when it is available to you. That friendly church and that kind man are two very good things that blessed both of our lives.

Notes to Stephanie: Days Remembered

The Day It Rained Green Chicken

Like most guys, I truly enjoyed gross humor. The day you told me about the parrot mass extinction at Kimmel was a day that should be recorded in the history of such humor.

To begin this tale, let us paint the picture of the scene that day. Years ago, a pair of parrots escaped from someone's house into the neighborhood around the school. These big green parrots started breeding. These non-native birds lived in communal nests that sometimes contained dozens of birds of all ages and rose vertically up utility poles. These nests became more numerous as did the birds. The school adopted them as unofficial mascots. No one harmed the birds, and they blended into the surroundings. But one day, it all changed—rather explosively.

The nests were filled with their excrement and waste. These fluids conducted electricity. And they did in that nest on the pole that fed power to the school. A short occurred early one morning, and thousands of volts of electricity flashed into the nest teeming with birds, just as kids and teachers arrived at school for classes. The intense heat flashed the fluids in the nest and in the birds themselves into steam , making the nest explode outward onto the grounds of the school's east side. Birds were cast outward with the debris for several yards. Many lay dead and literally smoking; some twitched in their death agony flash fried by the electrical bolts, while others were simply in pieces all over the parking lot.

Notes to Stephanie: Days Remembered

Amidst this sudden scene of carnage, little kids were walking through the debris along with their teachers—everyone in shock. The school building was dark; the power cut by the explosion. Some of the kids were upset seeing their school mascots laying about them roasted alive like fried chicken at some restaurant. I still remember your description of the field of dead birds and debris—some of the poor creatures were still smoking and scattered around the school. Later the school district called in people from maintenance to clean up the mess. The kids got sent home. While this event made the news, there were not any known photos or videos of the aftermath. Only the memories of those present that day can now recount this unusual tale.

When you told me all of this, I thought that when I was a kid we would have loved this as opposed to being upset like many of the kids were that day. All of us would have been overjoyed and would have laughed at the sight of the blasted birds and especially the darkened school. So what if dozens of birds died to free us from classes? It seemed the kids were more sensitive to things like that than we ever were.

So a darkened school surrounded by a lot of cooked parrots was the scene that day. What was really funny, was the fact that residents in that area trapped and ate the parrots, calling them "green chicken." Some of your students described that culinary fact to you one day. So a new way to cook green chicken was found, albeit using a recipe that would be very hard to repeat. But it was a dish worth remembering by people who enjoy weird humor created on "The Day It Rained Green Chicken."

Our First Thanksgiving

Our first Thanksgiving and Christmas together was marred by the ongoing trouble with my family over how we announced, or didn't announce, our wedding. So, that normally fun and family-oriented time was not very jolly indeed. Although, there were a few exceptions.

Our first Thanksgiving was funny when it was revealed to me that none of you had ever eaten smoked turkey and ham. In the past, you had bought a bird from the deli with the fixings or had gone out to eat since you were far from being a good cook. And that was always okay with me since I could cook well.

You and your kids told one especially funny story of how you had put a still frozen turkey in your oven. The result of that was an inedible bird and a trip back to the deli or a restaurant. Due to this lack of good food in your past during the holidays, I did what our family had almost always done on Thanksgiving. That was, I smoked both a turkey and a ham. At some point when I was little. We stopped roasting the bird or ham. I remembered when my dad bought his first smoker, and it changed forever how our holiday meals went. Our relatives had smokers also, so we all grew up having smoked fare.

Each year was a little different, but the general course of preparing the meal was the same. On the night before Thanksgiving, we built a fire at bedtime. The turkey went on the bottom rack and the ham on top. The drippings from the ham basted the bird. In the morning, they came off the fire and were sliced up; everyone wanted the crusty skin of both pieces of meat. It was served with homemade cornbread dressing

Notes to Stephanie: Days Remembered

(actually cornbread, biscuits, and stale bread), mashed potatoes, rolls, green beans, other foods of various kinds, and of course, many desserts. Such a menu was always good, satisfying, and provided good times with the family. So, I decided I would do the same thing for us all.

And that is exactly what we did our first Thanksgiving with a few minor differences in the side dishes and desserts. The best part of that meal was not the menu itself, but how good you and your kids thought the meat was and how surprised all of you were at having smoked ham and turkey. No surprise to me or my kids since that was what we knew. You and yours had never had such fare, and it evidently was a real treat for you all. Hence, we did the same thing on the Thanksgivings we were together. And I cooked other goodies at Christmas like prime rib or Beef Wellington to similar shock, surprise, and rave reviews.

In the end, Thanksgivings were always fun to me—the ones we had were no different. The family gathered around the table, ate a lot of good food, and enjoyed being together.

Those things are what we should always be the most thankful for—not material goods or the food itself. Things come and go in life, but our memories remain. Those memories are the meals we can always enjoy as we look back across the years, regardless of menu in front of us today.

Notes to Stephanie: Days Remembered

Our First Christmas and Thanksgiving with My Family

In contrast to the tension of our first holiday season, the second was good since peace had been restored, and things had returned to normal in the extended family. That was a good thing since past holiday times had been fun gatherings that were mostly without angst. The prospect of an ordinary Thanksgiving and Christmas was welcomed by all.

Within that new calm era, we did what our family usually did at those times. We rotated who hosted which holiday meal. He who hosted the day would smoke the bird or ham or provide the main course. Everyone else brought the supporting cast of this culinary theater: the dressing, desserts, veggies, and the dinner rolls. The person who hosted an event that year was not the important thing, however. The important thing was that we gathered as a family in a Norman Rockwell-like fashion as we did each year.

And we did exactly that on Thanksgiving and Christmas of that year. We ate, joked around, watched my mom get silly with some wine, and took some pictures of the clan. I remember one picture especially that was taken in front of my sister's at Christmas. We were all together in the sun in front of her house, and my arm was around you tight. We were all there in a line, smiling and happy, full from the meal, and content from the gifts. To me, that image showed everything about what a family holiday gathering should be like.

That feeling of being a family, whether it is by blood or by marriage, is more important than the food on Thanksgiving or the presents at Christmas. The real gifts we give to others, the things to be thankful for, are these times. Even though we enjoy and treasure these events, they seem to happen less as we get older and become more scattered—maybe because we have our own immediate families to tend to. But regardless of their frequency, they still provide part of the meaning of our lives. In part, they define who we are as persons and families even though the faces in the pictures come, go, or change as the years go by.

Bringing and Sending You Flowers

One thing I regularly did for you was send or bring you flowers. You always liked plants, greenery, and flowers, so I started doing that as we dated.

Sometimes, I would use the florist near your school if I was sending you some at work. Other times I would go to the grocery store and get some to bring to you on the way home. In any event, it was something that seemed to make you happy.

You would arrange them around the kitchen and leave them at work if I sent them there, many times to the jealousy of some of your fellow teachers. It seemed the ladies in the office always took a very long time to let you know I had sent you some. Were they admiring their floral beauty for their own sake or simply trying to spite you in some way? I do not know or care at this point, but there did seem to be a pattern connected with the delivery of flowers to you.

But what later saddened me was the fact that during our fussing, you told me to stop getting you flowers. It was hard on me that something you liked, and I had done out of my love for you, became something you resented. But I still brought them to you sometimes; I hoped it was a reminder to you that I still loved you and that I cared.

When we were getting divorced, a buddy of mine suggested over drinks one night that I should send some black roses to you at your school or your apartment over by the mall. He wasn't really serious, but even so, I would have never done such a thing.

I would not darken an innocent act that had once given us both color and brightness and had been done out of nothing but my adoration for you. I am reminded of the bouquets I gave you, since one of the plants I brought you is still alive in the kitchen by the sink. Its green leaves hang to the left and right as they always did, sloping in gentle curves down from its stalk by the window. That little green plant is one last memento of the others that were there before—one final allusion to gifts given in a love itself that was once bright and beautiful but now dark and lost.

Dinners with the Kids

Many times, we had our kids over for dinners at times that were not the holidays. I always cooked something everyone would like; we would talk, have some drinks, and dig into the feast.

Sometimes, we would have just your two over, along with your daughter's beau; and other times, we would have just mine. In some cases, we would have both sets of kids over. A full set of faces sat around your dining room table, and a copious amount of food was consumed.

I especially remember buying some good steaks at Kroger for your kids and your daughter's fiancé. Everyone was pleased at the result, and there was not a leftover steak to be seen when we were all done. Of course, I cooked other things over time as well; many of them were simple like chicken. Regardless of the menu, the real pleasure was having our kids over, especially when we had all of them over, and the entire family was assembled around us.

As time went on, having all of them over was increasingly hard. My daughter, being away at college, and your daughter's work made matching everyone's schedules to ours nearly impossible to do. The holidays were affected by this as well. There was no real way around that. Our kids were all grown, and they were living their own lives more with each passing day and month. We wanted to see them often, but we could not do that. Our broods, once young and dependent on us, had left the nest and were flying away from us to places we did not know.

That is the natural result of becoming adults, you see. In time, when they have their own kids, they will go through the same thing we did emotionally. They will love and long for their children to be near, still seeing them as young in the haze of memories past but also being proud they are grown and on their own. Sitting around their own firesides in some distant year, they will see their own little ones recede away from childhood into adulthood. They will perhaps realize then why we felt the way we did about them.

Jeffery W. Turner

Spending the Night at Mom's

Do you remember the time we went to my mom's and spent the night with her one Saturday? We drove out to Granbury one morning and spent some of the day around the square and eating lunch at Babe's. In the afternoon, we sat around her place and talked. That night, we had dinner. She made one of my childhood favorites, which was chicken breasts stuffed with crab meat, and it tasted as good as it always had. That night, she talked about things she did not usually share with people. But she did with you.

She told you things that non-family did not get to hear. That fact told me she liked and accepted you into the familial fold. It was not that other people didn't know those things, but she was not one to freely talk about them. She always moved on from things that were hurtful or unpleasant and did not dwell upon them.

I fell asleep that night on her couch, feeling very comfortable with how you and she seemed to like each other. Neither of you were tense with the other and chatted almost without end. You even called her "Mom"—something no one but my sister and I ever did. And thus, I felt that you had the mother that you never had. Your foster parents were certainly guardians: you said GiGi wanted to adopt you, but that never happened in the end. You were not adopted by my mom either, but you were in a sense since she treated you like one of us.

That is the way she is and always will be, you know. Regardless of our divorce, you did have a mom to talk to—at least for awhile.

Jeffery W. Turner

Playing Disc Golf as a Family

Disc golf, the fastest growing sport you never heard of, was one we started playing anyway. Most people have no idea what it is unless someone tells them about it, or they see it being played.

In the past, I knew about it from people I worked with back in the 90s, but I had never tried it. Then living here by the park, I noticed when the course was built, and disc golf started being played. As a result, we ordered starter sets with three randomly chosen discs.

We threw badly, but playing was a lot of fun with you and Jimmy. Heading down to the course to get some exercise after dinner was always fun, even though our scores were very,

very bad, and we all lost discs especially on hole #17, the so called "Beast." Indeed, that hole was a disk magnet, which daily sucked discs of the unwary into its watery maw.

Jimmy started mining the creek by the Beast's fairway for disks and found my favorite disk, the Instep Saturn, which I still use although I now have some 30 different disks from the usual manufacturers like Innova, Millennium, and DiscCraft.

The best parts of us playing were being able to get exercise and spend some time together. Those things were both fun and good. You even said as we divorced that you would miss that, too. I missed it, although I have found new people to play with. We play the old course, but we also play others as well; and I have learned about new discs to try from them. Regardless of the new courses I play or the new discs I buy, I still think the course in the park down the hill is my favorite. And the good old Saturn disc is still dependable, too.

So when I go down the hill and play the holes on the course, I sometimes think of our times there and how much fun they were. All families should find some activity that everyone will enjoy as we did and as my family did when playing volleyball in our backyard as a kid. Such things do more than keep one healthy. They also build memories and family ties, which are sorely missing in our modern age of mindless self-interest. And thus, a bunch of plastic discs thrown into the wind at the park, something simple and fun, built family memories for us all.

Swimming in the Middle of the Night

Having a swimming pool is a fun thing most of the time. One can jump in on a hot day after working in the yard to cool off or simply swim some laps for some exercise after work. Or you can sit on the steps of the pool under the shade and watch the clouds soar past overhead. When the family is over, all can join in the splashing while dinner is being cooked on the smoker nearby. Most of these activities are done in the daylight, so one might wonder if the pool can be useful in the dark. Indeed it can be used in the dark, and we did just that.

I remember more than once we were out there when the moon was full. The moon's rays shimmered down into the water, casting waves of silver and blue light across us and the yard.

When there was a breeze, the trees moved back and forth to the weather's rhythms, and their gentle swoosh matched the waves of light spreading in the pool. Certainly, such sites are nature's simple magic interacting with some of the mundane and everyday things man has made.

When there was no moon, we got in, too. I remember one night we woke up and could not sleep. We went out to the pool, and you cast off your nightgown and dove into the water bare as the day you were born. Naturally, I followed suit and was in the water with you. We swam and splashed around awhile, laughing and giggling at the same time to the sounds of the breeze above and were soon tired enough to go back inside and go to sleep.

Even now, I still go outside to watch the pool in

the moonlight or in the dark. Last night, I went outside and the moon was full again. The water shimmered and the trees once more swayed in the breeze as they always had before. With you gone, the only sounds were the swishing of the leaves in the wind, a distant voice in the dark, or the cars on the road—our talk and laughter was heard no more, except in my mind.

But regardless of how people change or come and go in one's life, the moon will always cast its soft, silver light down on us all. And the breeze will still rise up from the north or south, gently rocking the trees in its ageless arms while we hear its soft songs alone.

Jeffery W. Turner

The Watches You Gave Me

During the time we were together, you gave me three pocket watches: a gold one and two silver-colored ones with various chains on them to hook to my pants. You did this since I used to have a pocket watch my parents had given me one Christmas, but that had been stolen when my old house on the east side had been broken into. You knew I missed that watch; and you bought me the first one, which like the gold one I had lost.

I wore that watch to work many days, as you know, along with the wrist watch you gave me, too. And then you bought more—the two other pocket watches. One was for casual attire since it had a chain more like someone in a motorcycle club would wear. But it was a nice watch nonetheless. The other was one that could be worn with either casual or business attire and was neat, too. At that point I did have to ask you to stop buying me more watches. I really did not need more of them even though you wanted to find a real gold antique watch like someone from the 1800s might have worn. So in one year's time, you had bought me four watches, which I took turns wearing. When I wore one of them, I always enjoyed pulling the pocket watch out and checking the time like some old train conductor did in a western movie.

Today, I still have the four watches on my dresser, but now only one works. The wrist watch, the gold pocket watch, and one of the silver ones sit frozen at the time they stopped. I do not know if they simply need a new battery or if something is wrong with them mechanically, but I have not gotten around to getting them fixed. One day I will, and they will be restored, worn, and enjoyed proudly once more.

This set of pretty watches is an allegory for events in our lives. Something beautiful can appear in one's life; but later, there is a flaw that makes it stop being beautiful. This fact is true in relationships, too. What starts as "beautiful and brave," to quote the poet Rilke, sometimes develops problems that make it stop working the way the people involved wanted.

Perhaps, that is what happened to us, you see. Something that once was magical and good became broken and bad and thus on the dresser of life's memories like my broken watches silently do. The last watch working is but a reminder of what had been four watches ticking together, just as our memories show what once had been us as a couple in better times.

Notes to Stephanie: Days Remembered

Knick Knacks and Such

Most houses have knick knacks— little objects placed for decoration in the house. My house is no different. I have things from my childhood and also things you gave me—plus objects others have offered up, or I bought over the years.

From you, there is the samurai sword set, the tugboat from Goodwill, the two little abstract statues you said were a reminder of us as a couple, and a few other things here and there.

And there is the only wedding gift we ever got, which is the candy tray with the three Casper-like ghosts on it. That small thing was given to us by the folks around the corner, having the garage sale where you bought some beads. Hearing our story of just being married, they gave that to us as a wedding gift of sorts. Small and with little value, it was a gift nonetheless. And it was the only one we received when we got married. Of course, we asked people not to give us gifts, but it was the only wedding gift we ever got.

Regardless of their value or their source, knick knacks tell the story of your life in a way. They are not events recorded in a picture or a scrapbook, but they are a record of one's life just the same. The object itself is seen by many, but the meaning behind it is not—like with our one wedding gift. The thoughts, centered on these bits and pieces of things and tucked away in our minds, are what constitute the real meaning of all of these items accumulated over the years. These unspeaking possessions sitting on shelves and dressers are not noticed by many others, but they certainly could tell big stories about our personal histories if they ever were to speak to someone other than ourselves.

So, the little ghost-rimmed candy tray is one such thing. It certainly does not look like it recorded a wedding, but it does in my memories still. It sits even now with many other trinkets on my crowded bookshelves upstairs. Each gift or object there records events in my life that are both good and bittersweet, but all real and felt even now. And thus, the possessions arrayed there tell stories I alone will hear unless I choose to share.

Shopping For Clothes at Sears

One of the funniest things we ever did was when we were in the dressing room together at the Sears at Ridgmar Mall. I dare say not too many husbands do that with their wives. But we weren't like most couples, were we?

So one Saturday, you wanted to go shopping for clothes; and as usual, I went with you. We drove over to the west side of town to Ridgmar Mall and went into Sears. We went up the escalator to the women's clothes department, and you started looking for things you wanted to try on. While that went on, I simply sat down some place and watched people go by.

After awhile, you came with an arm full of outfits to try on. Without thinking, I followed you into the dressing room and shut the door. I did not notice that there were people who saw us go in there. I just sat down, watched you try on all of those outfits, and gave you my opinion of them when you asked. Of course, seeing you half-naked in your panties and bra was hardly something to complain about either. It certainly made me think of doing things with you other than shopping, but I digress.

When you finished going through the outfits, you gathered them up. We opened the dressing room door and stepped out. We paused as we suddenly saw the people outside looking at us with smiles or a questioning look. A man and woman coming out of a dressing room together is not something you see every day.

We both got a kick out of that when we realized what they were reacting to. Indeed, we did something funny without even trying.

And that is what made that little moment in time so memorable. Sometimes the best things come about when you are not trying to find them. Without trying, an event arises that creates a brief, intense moment of pleasure, joy, or humor that can make a regular day special. And that day in the dressing room was one of those times for us.

Notes to Stephanie: Days Remembered

Goodwill and Salvation Army: Adventures in Shopping

Perhaps one of the most interesting things I saw you do was to go shopping for clothes at the local Goodwill and Salvation Army stores. While you liked to shop at Sears, you liked these places even more. It was an adventure to you—a treasure hunt of sorts. You would search and search until you found something of value amidst the racks of discarded clothes around you.

When you were in those stores, you certainly had a system to your search. You considered only new things with a tag and things that were in style. You would go down each aisle, brushing through the tops, skirts, and pants and quickly evaluating the items for suitability. You were a woman on a mission—to find new stuff you liked at a low price. And you did that many times while I watched.

Two of your more memorable finds in the sands of retail archaeology were the Versace jeans and a pair of expensive shoes. I never cared for shoes per se—one pair of shoes was like another to me—but what I really liked were those jeans. A new $200 pair of jeans snagged for $10 or so if I remember right. And they simply looked fabulous on you. That one purchase was perhaps your greatest find in more than one way.

And thus, you regularly went to Goodwill and Salvation Army. Sometimes you found some good stuff, and sometimes you didn't find anything at all. But each time you did it, you had fun. Yes, I was bored out of my mind when I was with you on those hunts; but at the same time, I was always fascinated by your zeal for your quest and what you would unearth. On top of that, buying stuff there helped others out. Indeed, you were finding things to wear, but you were also helping put clothes on the backs of others not as fortunate each time you shopped.

That fact is actually the greatest treasure that came out of those many hunts for wearable goods. Being able to help yourself and others at the same time is perhaps the most valuable thing anyone can buy, regardless of what it costs.

The value of something is in the result it provides and not the monetary value society ascribes to it. That lesson was something you knew very well and practiced each time you went through those humble doors to buy or donate things. It is something that many others in our self-centered society should also learn. If they could, they would be enriched in ways that are beyond what they merely own.

Moving the Kids Out of Your House

Our biggest single crisis with our kids was deciding to move your kids out of your house and rent it out. There were a lot of reasons for this. Both of your kids had moved their significant others in without your approval, and finally, the huge $600 electric bill hit like a load of bricks. We first thought that letting them live there while they were in college would be a wise thing to do, but the situation had gotten out of control.

Of course, before your daughter left, we had to make Jimmy leave since we caught him doing drugs. Certainly, that period was a dark one for him, and we both know he grew up and straightened himself out into the good, young man he is today. And your daughter also matured after this period of time.

This period was the hardest time you had with your two (my hard time with my son was yet to come), and it troubled you greatly. You felt your kids had to stop depending on you and take responsibility for their actions. That was a hard thing for you to do, just as it was hard later to tell my kids some things. Our children had to learn what it was like to really live as an adult.

That is one of the hardest things for both parents and children to do. The parent is used to providing for the child's well-being, and the child is used to being taken care of. Therefore, kicking the little birds out of their nest is one of the hardest things to do.

Notes to Stephanie: Days Remembered

But you did it; and after an extended period of time, more wrecked cars, and other foibles, your kids crossed the great lifestyle chasm from being children to adults, who could take care of themselves. What originally hurt you so greatly was a good thing in the end that showed your great love for your children.

Jeffery W. Turner

The Trips for Jane

Besides working through CERT to help out with Ike, we were affected by the storm in another way. My daughter, who was going to A&M Galveston, had to hurriedly leave town when the campus was evacuated along with Galveston Island. Jane packed up some of her stuff, leaving her school books in her dorm room and drove in the sea of cars leaving Houston for our area. But that journey was only the first part of this odyssey.

After the immediate aftermath of the storm, the first question was: when could folks get back onto Galveston Island and the campus on Pelican Island? The campus was closed until further notice, and classes and students were moved to College Station and the main A&M campus. The bridge and causeway to Pelican from Galveston had been damaged by the storm and was impassible. However, a little destruction never stopped the Aggies, and a group of Aggie alumni in the construction business from Houston simply removed the debris and repaired the road enough so regular vehicles could drive onto the island. This was astounding since satellite photos clearly showed the damage that they dealt with.

The first journey for Jane was going to Galveston to get her stuff from her dorm. We drove down there with her and onto Galveston Island and Pelican, too. The damage was everywhere on Galveston Island, but Pelican Island and the campus looked unscathed. We went to her dorm and up to her room on the third floor, which did not get any water or debris damage at all. We marched up and down the stairs, carrying her stuff out. The truck was loaded, and we came back home, depositing much of her stuff in the garage.

While Galveston was made livable again, classes continued at College Station. Jane's mom moved Jane's stuff there for her. We did not have to be part of that. However, when the semester ended, her stuff had to come back home since classes would resume in Galveston next semester. That trip was done on a Saturday, and I drove there alone. After full day's work and I drove down 26 from Waco and went to her apartment that she shared with her suitemates from her Galveston dorm. I also met some of her friends—a few of which were exchange students from Norway. Remember the pictures I took of them? Like most young adults, they were full of life; and moving back and forth to Galveston was simply another adventure in life.

Notes to Stephanie: Days Remembered

Jane and I loaded up the truck, and we returned to Fort Worth, carrying some goodies like head cheese from the local H.E.B. We put most of her stuff in the garage; some of it is still there, by the way.

Then we went on the final trip: taking her stuff back to Galveston. Jane was already down there when we did that. Jimmy, you, and I piled the stuff in the truck and drove there, spending the night in Waco. The next day, we drove down 26 to 290 and went into Houston, driving by your old high school in Cy-Fair on the way. Then we arrived in Galveston, which was still far from being repaired.

We went to Jane's dorm; she was back in her old room again. We unloaded all her belongings and stayed the night on the island in a hotel that had not been heavily damaged. But there was still damage all around. Remember what we saw driving around the neighborhoods behind the seawall? Insides of house after house were in piles, lining many streets as far as you could see. The entire material part of thousands of people's lives was simply waiting to go to some landfill. Also, some houses or structures were simply not where they were before the storm. They lay askew from their foundations, awaiting collapse or demolition. How many lives were shattered by that storm? How many homes were destroyed or damaged beyond repair?

This was in contrast to areas along and on top of the seawall. While there was some visible damage in that area, most of it looked unscathed. This was because it was higher up, and the neighborhoods behind it that were lower had been hit by the storm's surge. While many businesses were still closed on the

Notes to Stephanie: Days Remembered

seawall, many were open again. In fact, do you remember eating at Landry's the night we were there? It was packed, just like the time we had been there before with Jane. It seemed from that narrow viewpoint that Ike had simply been a passing thunderstorm, and nothing had changed. Of course, that was not the case. As we were surrounded by that pleasant setting at Landry's, other not-so-lucky people lived in FEMA portable buildings next to their destroyed homes and dined on MREs and donated food.

We drove home the next day back to Fort Worth, but Jane and the destruction we saw were still on my mind. The day we went home was very pretty: bright sunshine with a few high cirrus clouds streaming in from the southwest. You could see forever up on the top of the causeway on I-45 because there was no haze or dust.

It was certainly a contrast to what Ike had been like. And that shows us something about life. It has its days filled with sunshine, and it has stormy days and times. Regardless of the weather you have to live with, we somehow take things in stride and can even enjoy the changes being thrust our way. The trips to see Jane at Galveston and College Station were such times. Amidst the destruction of Ike, we saw Jane, enjoyed a good meal, and were thankful that we were spared from the worst as so many others like us were not.

Notes to Stephanie: Days Remembered

The Lake Worth Albertsons

Late one afternoon, I went to the top of a hill near the house where I have a great view out to the west. On the horizon past the edge of the sea of houses, one can see structures in the distance. One can see the big grain elevators in Saginaw and more than one water tower sticking up, along with an oil drilling rig or two and a large highway sign. I glanced back and forth, taking in the view and trying to identify things I knew were there. One thing I did notice was the water tower at Lake Worth near your house.

Near that water tower, the kind that looks like an upside down onion with a stalk, is one place we had fun. That place was the Albertsons grocery store on Jacksboro Highway. A grocery store was a fun place? To me, it was, and here's why.

I remember trying to cook dinner at your place one night and going through your pantry and shelves to find spices and equipment. I saw your supply of these things was sorely lacking. Based on that culinary deficiency, I asked where the nearest grocery store was. You replied Albertsons or Wal-Mart on Jacksboro Highway. Preferring Albertsons, I went there and bought some food, spices, and even a couple of pots and pans. I went back to your house and prepared dinner.

As time went on, I kept doing that. I would drive over there—sometimes you would go with me—buy some victuals and prepare a good dinner. I even reorganized your cabinets some, so I would know where everything was.

Notes to Stephanie: Days Remembered

Since you did not cook, I did not think you ever noticed that. But that was okay; I enjoyed cooking for you and your kids. Plus it was a way for all of us to spend time together and get to know each other.

We went in Albertsons after you had moved to my house as well. When we went on drives up to Lake Country or elsewhere, we would drop in there and grab a six pack of beer and maybe a snack. That Albertsons, just an average grocery store, was certainly a part of our lives in more than one way.

And perhaps it still is. One day, I was driving home from somewhere on the west side. It was late afternoon on a clear, sunny day, and I did not know what I was going to cook. So I exited off of 820, went up Jacksboro Highway, and went into the Albertsons. Even though it had been months since I had been in there, maybe even a year, it still looked the same as it always had. The veggies and deli were to the left, the beer to the right, and all of the rest of the stuff was in the middle. The aisles were filled with the usual assortment of people from all walks of life, going back and forth with their carts and getting drinks, frozen pizzas, and the usual things people buy these days. The Albertsons hot French bread was of course present near the checkout lines as it was in the afternoon. All was as it had been before, and it seemed comfortable and familiar as always.

So I grabbed a cart and did the same thing they were doing, which was the same thing I had done with you. I walked the aisles, picking up something from the menu in my mind and remembered our days and evenings there. Finishing my shopping, I checked out, put the

Notes to Stephanie: Days Remembered

sacks in my car, and drove home and cooked my dinner.

Thus, I reentered a place I honestly thought I would never go into again. With grocery stores closer to my house, another Albertsons even, why would I drive 12 miles or so just to buy some milk or chicken? Honestly, I won't deliberately go there to buy food; but while I was there, I also went through the memories on the shelves of my mind— grocery bag from life filled with good and happy times spent in an average store. And that small bit of mental shopping was well worth the drive to Lake Worth that warm and pretty day.

Jeffery W. Turner

The Shoe Repair Guys: Mr. Holmes and Mr. Norrell

You had a couple of favorite pairs of shoes, which you had owned for several years. They fit you well, and you liked the way they looked. I had three pairs of boots, which I had more than once had resoled and fixed over the years. Why buy new stuff if the stuff you have is what you like?

Since these physical objects do wear and age like anything and everyone, they periodically need to get restored to their former condition. Thus with such footwear, one needs a shoe repair guy. And we both had our favorites. Each person was similar to the other, but like the clouds in the sky, they were not identical either. Both of our guys, Mr. Holmes and Mr. Norrell, had more in common than what they did not.

Like many such craftsmen they had small shops with old, worn, but working equipment. Their shops were in small buildings—nowhere near the usual bright, new shopping centers most people usually frequented. They saved money on overhead and were in places that had some character and history as well.

The personalities of the two men were a bit different. While both were friendly, they were not twins either. Mr. Norrell was more outgoing than Mr. Holmes who was a little gruff. As far as telling us when the work would be done, Mr. Norrell was a little vague while Mr. Holmes was more precise.

As far as money and things go, their prices were similar; repairing shoes had a market value just like anything else in our economy. The insides of their shops were not new, but they were not run down either. Both locations had the feel one gets when inside of an old building built decades ago. The décor was from an earlier era, which reminded me of something on old TV shows like *Andy Griffith*. Their places of business were perhaps artifacts of sorts—data for a cultural archaeologist to use in some history of commercial businesses and their structures.

These two men and their businesses tell us something about our culture. The media and politicians constantly espouse the idea of the small business and the people who own them. In our age of large corporations and mass retailing, such businesses are an island in a constantly rising sea of increased conformity and efficiency driven uniformity.

Contrasted with that modern reality, these two men are to be admired and also people to give one's business to. The money one pays for their services is worth far more than the utility they provide. The true value lies with what they do for us as a culture, which sprawls outside of their small doors in the endless strip centers of modern retailing. They provide a reminder to us that a person can do something on their own besides just be an employee of a Fortune 500 company like Wal-Mart. They show us that individual effort still makes a real difference, and that small businesses are something that should be valued for more reasons than just the services they supply.

Jeffery W. Turner

The Doll You Bought

One day when we were at the Will Rogers Flea Market, you spied an old, big doll. It was one of those dolls that came out of the 1950s or 60s. It was about two feet tall and had a dirty cream-colored dress. Its face and cheeks were dirty like the face of a little kid who had been out playing in the mud. You liked it, bought it, and took it home.

Once we got home, you put it on your dresser, standing upright with its eyes looking blankly out to the mirror on the opposite wall. She sat there for a short period of time until you began to remake her, to clean her up, and restore her to the beauty she once had when she belonged to a little girl whose identity shall remain forever unknown.

Notes to Stephanie: Days Remembered

You removed her little dress and washed it. You cleaned her skin and face like you did your own kids when they were little. I remember you standing her back up clean again. She was almost back to normal, but she lacked one thing—some proper hair.

When I lived on the east side of town, there was a doll store near my old house where I took my daughter. Jane would walk up and down the aisles, staring in little girl wonder at the many pretty, made-up dolls. I took you there one Saturday to look for a new mop of hair for your little doll—now looking almost new again.

Like my once little girl, you walked up and down the aisles looking at the dolls; it seemed you were looking for ideas on how to dress her up. Then you talked to the lady who ran the shop and asked if they sold new pieces of hair for dolls. They did, and you bought a brown wig for your doll and took it home.

You took the little hairpiece out of the box and put it on the doll. Then all at once she looked complete—remade and transformed from a dirty waif to the image of a proper young girl. She looked more alive than ever; her eyes no longer stared blankly now. She seemed to be almost animate with her pretty, new hair and her clean, long dress. She adorned our bedroom with her newfound glory—saved from perhaps being thrown out with the trash by someone who no longer wanted her.

The important thing about this series of events was not how well she cleaned up, but instead how you made the doll a metaphor for your own life. Like the doll, you described how you were discarded; but in the end, you had found belonging and beauty at last. In that way, you and the doll were one—perhaps even twins. Both of you were left by those who should have kept and treasured your beauty. Then later in life, others found you, saw your quiet grace, and cleansed away the layers of life's grit, so your natural splendor could be seen.

We should all hope that in our darkest hour someone will pick us up and wash away the dirty grime of existence that hides our shining, inherent glory and be given a new life, just as you gave one to that lonely and nearly forgotten doll.

King's and Crow's Liquor

Before I met you, I sometimes visited King's Liquors on I-20 and Old Granbury Road. You sometimes went into Crow's Liquor at White Settlement and 820. After we married, we went into Crow's on several occasions when we were out driving around or shopping. Both of those booze bastions were places I really enjoyed visiting. While I also liked going to the large chains like Majestic due to their selection, I really preferred the independents like King's and Crow's when I could go there.

And why was that? The big chains were typical fare on the menu of the American retail industry. They were huge, well-decorated, and full of stuff they were pushing or on special. Every location was very much the same for the most part. While the shopping experience at such places was good, there was nothing unique about it—there was no "art" in the soul of such a store, only the science of mass retailing.

King's and Crow's were the opposite of their more glitzy competitors. When you went into either of these stores, you were treated to something much different that harkens back to an earlier age in our commercial history. For starters, decoration and fixtures were minimal and functional. Sometimes beer and wine was simply stacked on the floor and wasn't on a shelf. The buildings were not in the endlessly multiplying strip centers in the newer areas of town. They were in older retail areas away from the rush of a mall or mixed-use development swollen with cars. In the end, they got your attention if you drove by since they were not hidden in the faceless, cookie-cutter forest of stores.

In short, such stores are unique. They are run by a family or by a sole proprietor who knows his or her merchandise. This type of store may be short on fancy décor but are long on customer service and good products.

This setting also brought back memories of the grocery store my dad's parents owned. It was small, not fancy, but it had the basics. And it had some character, too, like the back room, warmed by a space heater, where old men played dominoes each day. Such places, therefore, offered up more than just the goods they sold, they also brought us memories and stories to tell.

Hopefully, as our culture changes, this type of "mom and pop" outlet will see a new resurgence and become widespread once more. Such places are more than just a place to buy things at. They are a signpost of our community and its life, which provides much more than just a six pack of beer or a case of wine.

These individual fortresses of commercial activity, standing against the assaults of mass retailing's hordes, provide real enjoyment and even create memories one can value and treasure—unlike what one usually receives at faceless places like Wal-Mart and its everyday low prices. Thus, stores like King's and Crow's show you that price is not everything and that true value is measured in ways other than just dollars.

Jeffery W. Turner

Jane's Bad Grades, Roger's Good Grades

My daughter Jane, being a smart kid, could have made very good grades in college; but she started majoring in beer pong, let's say. Like many kids in college, the frosty mug appealed to her more than the cold, hard reality of getting her homework done. Thus, her grades started to slide most noticeably.

This was opposed to her brother Roger, whose grades had improved over the last year and who was now making the best grades ever. Roger seldom partook of the demon brew and did his homework before imbibing; there were fewer distractions and better marks in school.

This is an example of how young adults have to find their way in life. You can't make them study, but you hope they will. Sometimes, they must overcome personal difficulties or just get more serious about doing their work in school.

In that scenario, Jane is the latter, and Roger is the former. Jane is now working nearly full time and taking a full load of classes. She has gotten serious as a result of this regimen, and the tales of beer pong are fewer and fewer. Roger simply perseveres, is learning how to study better, and not get as stressed out about school.

We see a set of kids growing up, forever leaving the carefree world of their childhood behind. They have to do the work themselves, and that is a good thing. Overcoming life's trials and tribulations, while acquiring discipline and resolve, will give them the skills to be good parents one day and also help them

Jeffery W. Turner

succeed in the game of life we started playing when we were young like them.

Notes to Stephanie: Days Remembered

CPA and CFA: They Aren't Professional Designations

Do the letters CPA and CFA mean something to you? Do they mean Certified Public Accountant or Chartered Financial Analyst? Not in this case. Instead they mean Citizen's Police Academy and Citizen's Fire Academy. Two classes the people of Fort Worth can take to learn about their police department and their fire department. We took both. .

With us both being in CERT, it was a natural thing to do since many of the same folks who are in CERT or Code Blue take the courses out of curiosity or community service. We took them out of the former more than anything; plus we thought it would be fun to do.

So, what did one do in these classes? The mission of the classes was to educate the public on what police officers and firemen did, from a mostly hands-on viewpoint. In the CPA class for example, we got to go on the police firing range and shoot pistols or AR-15 rifles on the range. In CFA, an example of the hands-on experience was visiting the fire station at Alliance Airport and driving around in a fire truck while there. There was also a lot of class time that explained the department's missions, procedures, and other relevant topics. In short, both classes were miniature versions of what recruits went through when they joined one of the departments. And in both classes, you went through a graduation ceremony and got your picture taken with one of the chiefs.

We really enjoyed taking those classes. It was one of the most fun things we ever did since it was something we did together and had a joint interest in. Plus, it was free. Like our previous CERT class where we met, it was an example of how members of a community can learn more about their government, do some community service, and have some fun as well.

Based on what I experienced, I feel such things are a wise use of our tax money. It is a shame that with the current budget ills, the classes are on hold. Perhaps, when the economy is better, this will change and more eager legions of people, following the "Fort Worth Way," can learn more about the men and women who serve their fair city nestled on the bluffs of the Trinity, enjoy themselves, and help the place they call home.

Jeffery W. Turner

Touring the County Jail and Homicide Night

Do you remember the Citizen's Police Academy class? Being in CERT, we got to sign up for that class and learn more about the training Fort Worth Police officers received and the things they did in their jobs. The topics we were exposed to varied from firearms to traffic operations. But the two nights we found most interesting, and also shocking, were the evenings for the Tarrant County Jail tour and Homicide Night.

Now, dear readers, if you can't stand graphic or gross things, please go on to the next note. What I am about to tell you is 100% true, but it also might make you ill. So, be warned.

Notes to Stephanie: Days Remembered

Touring the jail was something else indeed. We took police vans up to the jail and assembled in a room. A deputy then prepared us for the tour. The lecture was simple enough, but the real horrors were not seen until we were deep in the bowels of the jail. And horror was the word that applied to some of the things we learned.

As we walked through the old and new parts of the jail, we were told that the prisoners would throw their feces on the guards, try to stab them, and eat cockroaches crawling on the floor. One deputy said it still made him sick to recall the crunching sound of the cockroaches being chewed. Next, we learned of the "crapper phone," the way prisoners talked to each other through the commode and the pipes like a telephone. Using that calling plan had the added bonus of getting infections by touching the bottom of the bowl. Next was the tale of the female inmates ingesting sausages into an orifice other than their mouth, —again getting an added bonus of an infection. (The kitchen was told to chop up the links.) Then, there was the black prisoner masturbating in front of the ladies as we all walked by. Thank God I missed that display. All the while, we were expressly told NOT to touch the walls of the jails for fear of contaminates there. In short, the tour was informative and also horrific at the same time. It made you swear that you would never have to go there under arrest.

After the delights of the jail, we next encountered the joys of Homicide Night where FWPD detectives showed real pictures of victims of murder and manslaughter. We saw things you would expect—spouses blown asunder by shotgun blasts of their mates, people sliced apart by knives and machetes, people stabbed so many times they looked like human

Swiss cheese, and other evidence of real crimes in our city.

But the topic that got most people's goat was the nurse who died while masturbating in her shower. She strangled herself to death the way the actor David Carradine did. The detectives talked about this with no emotion as they showed us the slides—the nurse sitting slumped over straddling her bathtub with a noose around her neck and a large red self pleasuring device protruding from her loins. All in a day's work, they said. *"Just the facts ma'am. Just the facts."* They showed little emotion while they showed us their job.

All of these scenes showed things our first responders deal with each and every day. They get paid less than many of us do but deal with blatant evil and acts of human depravity few of us will ever see. But amidst these horrors and wickedness, they remain human just like we do. They do their jobs, tend to their families, and walk their dogs. Somehow, they put away the evil they see, so they can remain normal like the rest of us.

In that, they are perhaps our society's greatest citizens. They put up with so much, but receive so little, just so citizens like us can go to a class, see the immorality and crime we refuse to deal with unless we are a victim of, and return to our quiet homes in the nicer parts of town. Perhaps, we hear the wailing sirens of their work in the distance late at night when we are safe in our warm, little beds. We sleep safely due to their tireless efforts. We should be thankful for their work and that we only see the filth they deal with in a class.

Notes to Stephanie: Days Remembered

Buying our Wedding Rings

When we were planning our wedding, we decided to spend as little possible and keep the affair simple. This choice also applied to buying our wedding rings, as you know. We ruled out from the start going to some full price store like Zales and paying thousands of dollars for an overpriced ring. We wanted to save our money for something else like a honeymoon or buying a house together.

Based on that, we started looking for rings at places that most people never set foot in—laces like pawn shops and stores that had used jewelry as well. We found your ring at a pawn on the west side near the base. It was a ring set made of white gold and diamonds that you immediately loved. Even with its appeal, we looked around some more; but you soon decided that was the one you had to have on your finger. So one day after work, I went and bought it, sequestering it away in my game room in a box for our wedding day.

You searched more for my ring after I bought yours. You found one you thought I would like. Since I didn't wear rings and jewelry, the look of it was not so important to me. One Saturday, we went to a store out by Hulen to view my ring. I immediately loved it, contrary to my dislike for jewelry. The ring was a white and yellow gold with three diamonds on it, set atop a simple, modern-looking design. You said the three stones stood for: "I always loved you. I love you now, and I will always love you." I was sold, so you bought the precious, little ring and took it home to your house.

Notes to Stephanie: Days Remembered

On our wedding day, we, of course, put our rings on with happiness and pride. I always liked the look of mine, and you said you loved yours, too. From the time we were married, I wore my ring; I rarely took it off. It became part of me, just as you became part of my life. The ring and I were one, just as you and I had become that way, too.

But as time went on, we lost our love. We got divorced, and I wore the beautiful ring no more. It sat upon my dresser until one day, I went to a pawn shop in Watauga and sold it, having shed a tear or two before I went.

In a way, the act of buying and wearing our rings symbolized the start of our marriage. The act of selling mine signaled the end. But since you bought it at a pawn shop and I sold it at one, that small act of sad closure perhaps signaled the start of someone else's marriage. Just as I first saw and wore my ring that once adorned another man's wedding finger, my ring someday might be worn with love by someone else. In that way, something good, driven by the true love of other people we won't ever know, will come in spite of the sad way our time together ended. In that way, my pretty ring with its three bright diamonds I loved so much will find a new home and hopefully will not be removed again to be sold in another sad ending of time with someone once loved.

Notes to Stephanie: Days Remembered

Loving in the Pool

Neither of us is in to inappropriate public displays or actions that would seem improper, but one day we did something that I never thought we would do.

One day in the summer, we were in the pool on a Saturday or Sunday afternoon. We had been drinking some, and we were both a bit tipsy. Not drunk, but we were leaning to the side of thinking we were invisible. We started getting frisky with each other; and without much hesitation, the bathing suits came flying off. Soon, we were making love by the step on the north side of the pool by the fence and bushes there. It is one thing to do that in the dark, which we also did, but in broad daylight is another thing entirely. Lucky for us, the trees, the fence, and the geometry of the houses meant no one could see us doing The Wild Thing.

Soon, we completed The Act, got our suits back on, and laughed about it later as we sobered up. Even better, the neighbors did not see us, did not complain, or call the police. You having been in Citizens on Patrol/Code Blue and both of us being in CERT would have made being arrested for public lewdness even worse. We were probably lucky, you know. Oh well, it was fun and one of the special moments that we had together, albeit one caused by the "demon brew" on that hot afternoon. Certainly, it was hot in more than one way, but we won't go into details about that here.

This goes to show that sometimes things just happen; you do something you never thought you would do, but later realize that you did do it with some surprise. Hopefully, you remember the event in question with some fondness and laughter as well. Such inadvertent acts are part of what make us human after all. And as long as you don't go to jail or get hurt, they are a good thing in the end. They should be treasured as much as some deliberate act of greatness that we are more apt to share with others. Their effects, while sprouted from spontaneity, are just as important as things we planned to do. So the next time you do something you thought you wouldn't do, just forgive yourself and go on to life's next adventure—perhaps in a swimming pool.

Jeffery W. Turner

Fun in Fredericksburg

One the way home from one of our trips to Laredo, we spent a night in Fredericksburg. That town, like Kerrville, is one of the jewels of the Texas Hill Country. If you go there, it will not take you long to see why so many people like that little burg and go there on a regular basis.

Fredericksburg is one of the many German settled towns in that part of the state. That ethnic heritage is still alive and well to this day. You can walk down the main drag and see German restaurants along with other businesses whose names imply that they are Deutsche Volk owned and operated.

The German flavor of this town is not the only thing about it that gives it its flavor. Along with places that have German food or wares, there are also places that show the Texan side of the culture there. One example is the store where we bought salsa and beef jerky. Those two things are certainly signature items that tell a person that they are not in New Jersey.

And let us not forget history as well. How many people know that famous Admiral Chester Nimitz of World War II fame was from Fredericksburg? Probably not many who are not into history. But he was, and there is a large museum there in his honor. Next to it is the more recent Museum of the Pacific War. If you are into World War II, you can certainly get a full helping of that historical meal when you are Fredericksburg.

Finally, there is the countryside itself of the Hill Country. There are hills of granite and limestone threaded by clear streams with horses, cattle, and goats grazing nearby. The flora is sparse in places, but you can see a long way when there are few trees. While our eastern cousins may not see the grandeur of this region, it is a magical place to many who live in the Lone Star State.

All in all, Fredericksburg is a place worthy of a visit. Going there with you was one of the most fun things we ever did. The variety of things we saw, ate, and did made for a wonderful weekend and provided a much deserved break from the chaos that was still rampant in our lives. That weekend told us that when things were going a bit crazy, couples should go on a weekend "Great Escape" and wiggle their way through the barbed wire that entangled our everyday lives so much in our modern time.

Notes to Stephanie: Days Remembered

The Bridge over I-35W at Heritage

As you might remember, I like places with a large and expansive view of the country side. Most of the time, I found these places on a farm road out in the country—but not always—sometimes they were found close to home. One such place was the bridge over I-35W on Heritage Trace near the hill at Heritage we sometimes visited.

When you went across that bridge going west, you were on top of a hill overlooking the rolling landscape that curved up and down to the south. You could not see east or west due to the topography, but you could see a large field of view looking southward. Most of the central part of Tarrant County was in view, along with part of southwestern Dallas County as well.

We would drive across the bridge, and you could see the spires of downtown on the horizon, the huge grain elevators at Saginaw, and other landmarks that defined what Tarrant County physically was. We were both almost breathless at this site—few places nearby afforded such a vista that spanned so much physical space and showed so much of our local geography.

Seeing the shape of the Earth and man's coating of houses, buildings, and signs made you appreciate how big a city can be and the variety of objects that fill its borders. More than once, we both pointed to something on the horizon or gestured to some place closer, and we remarked about what was around that point. We were like explorers looking at a map for important places; but in this case, the map was not made of paper. It was made of the reality in front of our eyes. Regardless of the allegory, it was a very personal thing to do since we were viewing places that had been part of our lives for many years.

In a way, this place was a scrapbook of sorts. Each thing we could see had a story to tell. Each building, field, or highway we saw from there recounted something about us, like a Kodak picture would do.

And as life changes, so does the view. New houses are built, a new skyscraper is launched towards heaven, or something simpler like a new billboard or gas station appears. The view always changes, as does a scrapbook when new pictures are added to its pages. Thus these vistas, like a set of pictures, can tell us whom we are and where we have been.

Jeffery W. Turner

Another View of Forever

One day not so long ago, I went to Bonds Ranch Road to see the "View of Forever." It was a very sunny, but cold day, with a little wind from the north. I got there about 2:30 in the afternoon. There were a few streams of high clouds coming out of the southwest—a perfect day to gaze into the distance since the air was so clear.

I sat there thinking about things; and once again, I noticed just how much you can see from up there. In the distance some ten miles away, I could see Loop 820 turn to the southwest towards White Settlement—the sun was reflecting off of the cars and trucks, which could be seen even that far away. The horizons were sometimes fifteen miles away; parts of three counties were within view with their

Notes to Stephanie: Days Remembered

rolling terrain sloping to infinity and beyond. With such vistas, you could imagine yourself as an omnipotent god looking down from afar at the mere mortals going about their journeys.

Somewhat closer to me, you could see the water tower at Lake Worth, which is not so far from your house, sticking up over one of the hills to the south. Downtown could also be seen in that general direction—the skyscrapers pointing to heaven above the streets where we had walked hand in hand more than once.

And closest of all was Lake Country Estates, which was your favorite place to go to when you were looking at real estate. From my vantage point, you could see some of the places we had driven by. You could see the back of the strip center where we once bought some beer and areas of houses, such as the ones along the road on the ridge overlooking the rolling terrain to the north, including Bonds Ranch Road. Just like the view of 820, you could see the sun reflecting off of the cars going north and south on Boat Club Road.

This day was like one that we had spent together there once, and I listened to the pretty, but melancholy, song that was the theme from the movie *Gran Torino*. On that sunny day nearly three years ago, we had sat on the top of the hill, looking at the View of Forever and saw those same things together: the glint of faraway cars and the shapes of houses all framed by the sky, the clouds, and the bright light of the sun on a cold day. We sat there marveling at the sight and talked about our lives, and what was going on at the time. Together, we were at a place that seemed so far from the things that were weighing on us at that the time—a place surrounded by beauty and the endless sky that arched above us. We had a brief moment of peace and contentment there on a pretty day now long ago.

And then I came back to the present as the song was still playing. I gazed back to Loop 820; the glints of reflected sunlight seemed to flicker to the rhythm of the ghostly piano rifts in the song. Then it was still; nothing was heard; the song had ended. Only the wind was heard; there were no cars going down the road; and for a moment, there were no flashes of light from the distant cars. Time had stopped it seemed, and all was well even though you were not there with me. But that fine moment also ended like all such times do.

That time and place tells us many things about life. Life can be swirling around us; some things are close to us, and some are not. Events come and go at random—their frequency and severity ebbing and flowing ever constantly.

And then briefly, it all stops. Life is frozen around us, and all is quiet for awhile. The calm is all too brief as the cycle once more begins, and the flickers of experience once more appear in the distance. All set within the frame of time's large window, like what I saw from the "View of Forever" one quiet winter day.

Notes to Stephanie: Days Remembered

We Like Luby's

Nowadays, most people who dine out go to some flashy restaurant chain, whose advertisements are constantly seen on TV and championed by some celebrity who endlessly tells you how hip you are if you dine there. Besides such obvious media swill, you are also told how fashionable and unique their food is. Sometimes, that is true; but in this sea of constant ad pitches, one can forget that there are simpler alternatives out there, which are not framed by a glitzy TV commercial and also have very good food. What is one such alternative you ask? A cafeteria like Luby's.

Yes, a cafeteria—some place your parents or grandparents might have taken you for lunch after church one Sunday. A place where people who are not hip or cool go to get everyday food.

Indeed, everyday food. Chicken fried steak, fried chicken, Salisbury steak, baked and fried fish, green beans, mashed potatoes with more than one choice of gravy, and more timeless things even like a carrot salad or Jell-O. All these dishes provided a cornucopia of choices that seemed to be like something from the 1960s rather than something you would expect to find in the early 21st century where the likes of Thai, bistro, and vegetarian food are seen more and more.

While we both enjoyed non-everyday fare, Luby's was still one of our favorite places to eat. We ate there on nights before you had school functions and on the weekends for a bountiful lunch on a Sunday when I did not want to cook. We both enjoyed making our choices while going down the line and sitting down to consume our meal. It was not fancy or trendy, but it was always tasty and predictable. Plus, it was not expensive. It was affordable good food anyone could partake of, and partake we obviously did.

Eating there also brought back a flood of memories of eating at places like that with my mom, dad, and sister as a kid. There were later times with my own kids, too, who also liked cafeterias. You had similar memories from your childhood as well with GiGi and Charlie. To us, Luby's was a family place more than most modern chain restaurants were.

Why was that so? I think it was the setting more than anything. You were not distracted by an overly friendly waitress, loud music, smoke from the bar, or TVs endlessly showing sports or mindless reality shows. Instead, you were focused on each other and talking, like when you sat at your own table at home. Family talks like that built closeness and created fond memories when conducted around a common meal.

And like those domestic gatherings, a table at Luby's did that, too. In a way, it was almost like home to me, you, and many others—judging by the throngs seen there.

Home, or something like it, is always a good thing—, a place that should be there for people to gather at, enjoy a table of good, familiar food, and just talk to each other without much distraction.

Notes to Stephanie: Days Remembered

Modern chain restaurants are impersonal and full of hype. Places like Luby's are not that way, but they are seen less and less as time goes by. From my cultural and culinary viewpoint, that is a shame. As places like Luby's slowly vanish, we are losing something that is good for us as people and also good for our stomachs. Let us hope they will remain with us to create more fond memories of each other, our families, and of course, the good food.

Jeffery W. Turner

Driving Through Riverside

I always liked the times we drove through Riverside on the east side of town. It was a neighborhood built in the 1930s, I think. Older and not flashy it is to this day. The style of its homes was something literally from the time of our parents and grandparents— something from a movie like *The Best Years of our Lives*. And like that movie we both enjoyed, we liked going through that part of town.

It was a place that looked stately, but also it showed the wear and tear of time on its facades. The rows of homes stretched north and south on the bluff overlooking the Trinity River; the geography was its namesake as much as its location. The many trees gave it a look unlike the cookie-cutter pods of new houses some miles to the north outside of the city's core. It was an island universe of sorts, like many neighborhoods are, having its own unique set of people, businesses, and stories to tell.

It was not a wealthy area of town. The businesses reflected that. There were no fancy strip malls or chain restaurants to be seen—just drive-in groceries selling beer and fast food, some ageless mom and pop stores, and the various residential and commercial homesteads of urban pioneers who decided to move there with hopes of renewal and change.

Like many older neighborhoods, it had its own character. It was a part of town many never went to or had forgotten about entirely, but it was still known well by those who called it home or knew something of its history.

When you and I drove through there, we knew those things, especially since you drove through the area daily to get to work. We both saw its faded past and also saw what others were trying to do to make its future bright. That mixture of the old and new urban change made a drive through Riverside enjoyable and fun. It gave us a sense of both the past and a glimpse of what might be seen by future generations, who might one day drive through there and wonder what it was like before, just as we did so many enjoyable times before.

Notes to Stephanie: Days Remembered

Tornado Sirens in the Dark

One of the things that make living in Texas interesting is the weather, especially the storms that arise to lash us in the spring. With each passing storm front, you are given a show full of nature's fireworks and surprises. Each performance is different; each has something new to show. And one night, there was something fresh to see or hear, I might say.

That early spring night was like many others. It was humid and cloudy, and the storms were coming towards us. A strong squall line was tracking in from the west where storms are usually born. The Weather Service had posted numerous warnings and watches for severe thunderstorms and some tornadoes as well. I went in and listened to the NOAA Weather Radio to hear the storm reports and new warnings, which inched their way to Tarrant County and Fort Worth. As my dad once said, "Someone was going to catch some hell that night." It appeared we were next.

You weren't there when this was happening; you had a function at school. I had spoken to you before it started and told you about what was coming from the west. As the evening wore on, your program ended, and you called to tell me you were on your way home. You were just in time for the storms to sweep across our part of the world. And that they did.

Storms are not unusual in North Texas; but sometimes, some of the events that are around them are a bit different, and this was one such night. Like a scene in some movie, it became calm and still outside. There was no wind, and the clouds overhead streaked from the southwest at high speed. In the distance to the west, one could hear the low, rolling growl of thunder sweeping across the rolling prairies and hills to the west. Sometimes, a sheet of lighting would be seen illuminating the cloud deck above the quickly fleeing scud clouds below. The calm was the most noticeable; you always heard that if it was calm before a storm, something bad was on its way. A tornado was near, the old timers would tell you.

That old tale was about to become true, it seemed, when I first heard the tornado sirens fire off far to the west. Usually, you heard the siren in the neighborhood on the top of hill one half mile way, but not this time. The sounds in the distance were being blown to the threshold of hearing by the wind coming from the west, which had picked up again. The wind and the siren's wale made you think that people miles away were in the path of destruction and doom.

The sounds grew louder as another belt of sirens

nearer to the house, but still not the ones nearby, were set off by Fort Worth Emergency Preparedness. The mental image in my mind was that the storm's edge, or the violent swirl of a large tornado, was inching its way eastward towards us—the sirens being sounded as this angry weather woe approached.

I called you again to tell you this and to see where you were. You were not far from the house; you could see the storm with its large bolts of lightning very clearly just to the west of I-35W. The rain was not far behind it. You beat the storm to the house, and the final interesting event took place. That is, the local siren finally went off. You could no longer hear the ones in the distance, just the one up the street from the house wailing and accompanied by loud cracks of thunder. It seemed that the meteorological monster was about to stomp its way to our very door. The high tide of the storm's wave was due

Notes to Stephanie: Days Remembered

to strike at any time.

Not much longer after that, you drove up to the house, and the rain started. You were safely home; and in the end, the storm was not so bad. Indeed, there was a lot of thunder, lightning, wind, and rain; but no tornadoes were actually seen near us. The storm was not as severe at our home as it was west of there. Thus, the sirens were sounded for not it seemed, their cries of warning heralded not the thing they were supposed to advise us about. But that was okay. No one was hurt, and the show itself was ghostly, fearful, exciting, and magnificent all at the same time. The waves of tornado sirens going off and the wave of storms provided another night of free entertainment to those people willing to watch its performance and notice how unique weather can sometimes be even when set on a stage of what is familiar and expected.

Jeffery W. Turner

The Kid Working Alone

Sometimes a small act of service or kindness deserves a big thank you. And the day I got some chicken wings at a place across from the Wal-Mart Super Center was one of those times.

One Saturday, we were out shopping and went into the Wal-Mart Super Center on Beach Street. We went inside, bought stuff, and got back into the car. At that point near midday, my blood sugar started to get a little low, and we hurriedly looked for a place to get some lunch. Across the street was a wing place. That sounded good, so we drove over there.

We went inside, and there was just one person working—a teenage boy. I ordered some wings, and he started working on the order. He apologized for no one else being there and assured me that the order would not take long since I advised him that my sugar was getting low.

He went into the back, got some wings, and started cooking. The phone rang, too, and he talked to customers calling in orders to pick up. He was doing the work of two or three people and was juggling things around. He looked a bit harried, but he kept his focus and soon my wings were done. He thanked me for being patient, and I thanked him as well.

Afterwards, we talked about how polite he was and how he did not stop caring, like so many young people do now. He was a breath of fresh air in a stale environment of the common bad and shoddy customer service nowadays. I was thankful for what he did—a small act of service and kindness for someone he did not know.

As the saying goes, one good turn deserves another, so I made a point to give him some thanks as well. I looked up the website of his restaurant chain and found the customer comment section. I sent in a detailed thank you for that young man whose name I did not know, but whose face I can still picture simply because he was polite and helped me out.

I never got a reply from the company he worked for, and I never saw him again. Once I thought about going to see if he was there and had received the thank you, but I never did.

Regardless of knowing the name of that Good Samaritan, who was just doing his job, such small acts of kindness make an impression on me. For whatever reason, these acts tug at my heart and fill me with emotions that are hard to explain. Regardless of their source, they should be noticed and repaid in some way; that is the essence of the Golden Rule, you know. If we did such things for each other, especially for strangers, our culture would be a far friendlier place for us all. And that would be the finest thing we could serve to one another in a time of need.

Jeffery W. Turner

Your Little Classroom

When you started at ISD when we were dating, I was amazed at the room they put you in and had the nerve to call a "classroom." It was not really a room, but a big closet. It wasn't the usual place a teacher was placed in with as many kids as you had in your pull-out sessions. But it was yours nonetheless.

The principal told you there were no other rooms available due to overcrowding and that you would have to make do until something better was found. Being the resourceful person you were, you set out to make your space useable and comfortable for your kids.

I remember more than one Saturday going there with you to put up things on the walls that helped you teach lessons to your kids. We

Notes to Stephanie: Days Remembered

rearranged things in the small space, taped words and letters on the walls, and sorted out lesson plans and handouts. Plus, we put gummy bear treats in jars that you used for rewards. All in all, we made an area that never should have been used as a classroom into just that.

Over time, you went in there every school day, taught reading, and worked with many kids who needed your help so badly. Many of them improved, and their test scores went up as well. Your little classroom, while small in size, generated results that were very large. Many lives were touched by your great work in that cramped space. The kids were helped regardless of the size and shape of the room. Your students benefited, in spite of its dimensions, by your considerable talent and great care.

In that light, we should remember that the image of a place is not the reality of it. Instead, the true nature of a thing is provided by the actual results obtained from it. Your little classroom was one such place—small in size but big in what it provided for others who needed some help.

Notes to Stephanie: Days Remembered

Coco and Chocolate

With you being half French, it was natural that you liked the Coco soap and lotion by Chanel and that movie titled *Chocolate*. Those two things were a small snapshot of whom you were.

The soap was special to you. You had used it since you were in college and always had some around. The wonderful thing about it was how it mixed with your body chemistry; your pheromones interacted with it to give you a fine scent from head to toe. You didn't need to wear any perfume, I thought (although you usually did that, too).

What was interesting about this magical stuff was the annual quest you went through to get it. A quest I joined after we were married. Chanel only made so much of it, and it was available only near Christmas. Stores received only a small quantity of the authentic product, and you had to go to more than one store to get a year's supply of it. And that is exactly what you and I did. We went to Dillard's, Foley's, and elsewhere to find a bar here and there. I even ordered some online from Neiman Marcus once. So after a long process, there would be enough to last you until the next year came.

Now the movie *Chocolate* was another thing entirely. It was your favorite movie. It was in French and English, but you watched it in French, repeating the dialogue as the actors spouted it out. The plot of the movie was something you identified with; the leading actress was a version of you and your life. That similarity was probably the reason you enjoyed it so much. You saw your own story in the plot of the movie. There did seem to be some parallels; I think you would agree. But not totally—as fiction and fantasy did not equate with reality. Regardless, you were drawn to that movie and truly enjoyed watching it each time you viewed it.

Personally, I could not stand the movie; but I usually said to go ahead and watch it anyway when you wanted to view it. Normally, we watched it in the bedroom where I could mercifully fall asleep and not be tortured by the storyline. But we each had our favorite flicks, didn't we? You did not like some of my favorites either. But I digress now and have drifted off from making my point.

So, what then is the point you ask? The point is that there are little things that tell us whom we are. Some of these things are mundane, like the Coco soap. Others are more visible, such as a movie loved. Regardless of the thing or whether or not someone can see it, external objects we like are a sign of the type of person we are.

So when you watch a movie with a person, pay attention to the plot since the story being told might tell you what his or her own tale is. Or the next time you are in a store with that person, watch what kind of soap he picks up since it may be the thing that cleans away the dirty mystery of whom he really is.

Peach Ice Cream on 281

On our way back from Fredericksburg and Laredo on our mini-honeymoon, we started craving peach ice cream. I do not remember exactly why we did; I think it was because we saw peach orchards alongside Highway 281 and started drooling. Thus, we started looking for a place to stop and get a sugary, cold batch of its goodness.

As the miles went on, we did not see a place after we decided to get some. We looked left and right as we drove through the hills, but didn't see a place that offered it. But suddenly we came to Johnson City, and there was an abundance of riches along the way. One place after another advertised its presence—each beckoning us to stop. Finally, we spotted a little stand next to a café and pulled over. We got out, and there was the pink, creamy treat we searched for. Even though my diabetes said no, I said yes to buy some.

We got back in the car and drove off north, devouring the cold, peachy goodness. Bite after bite, we savored its taste and texture. Mile after mile, we enjoyed the pleasure it brought. And then it was gone, locked away in our tummies to be digested on top of the Church's fried chicken we had earlier in Lampasas.

While the time spent eating that icy treasure was brief, I still remember how it tasted. It was sugary and fruity--an instant of culinary bliss. Thus, that dish was like some things in life—it was short and sweet. But those moments, while fleeting, are the ones that sometimes satisfy us the most.

Winscot Road

One place I always liked to go was Winscot Road, which is southwest of town and is actually named Winscot Plover Road. Before I knew you, I went there from time to time to enjoy its rolling pastures, the view of the sky, and the sound of the wind blowing through the grass. It was one of the places most people did not know about or never saw while passing through to somewhere else.

It was a place that looked like it was locked away in a time decades long past. The prairie there rolled up and down across fields with hardly a tree. If you looked west, you wouldn't see a house at all, except a couple where the ranch hands live. You could think you were hundreds of miles away from any city or town—a place populated by more cattle and horses than people.

On a bright winter day with some high clouds streaming above, you could just as easily have been in Wyoming or Montana—half a continent away. But you weren't; you were just a few minutes from downtown Fort Worth and the sea of houses spreading from its center.

With these images in my mind from those prior visits, we went there one Sunday afternoon on one of those pretty winter days I enjoyed so much. We drove there in the pickup and had a six pack of cold beer tucked away.

When we arrived, we pulled over at the top of my favorite rise on the blacktop road alongside the railroad track. I rolled down the windows, and we sat there sipping a beer. The wind blew gently, and there was no one around. No radio, no TV, no people—just the sky, the clouds, and us.

We enjoyed some time there talking, but also just looked in silence at the scene that could have been from a western movie with John Wayne. We were part of a pastoral scene from another time. Cattle were slowly grazing in the pasture beneath the blue and white speckled sky with not a living person in sight.

We melted into the surroundings and were part of what was there in front of our eyes. We were no more important than a strand of barbed wire, a blade of grass, or a lone mesquite tree up on one of the rolling hills. For a short time, until we drove back home, we were part of Winscot Road.

Places like that teach us something. They show us that we are part of something bigger than ourselves, and that many things we hold dear are not permanent. What remains after we leave this life is the earth, the sky, and the creatures that dwell there—all oblivious to the cars, TVs, and shopping malls that loom so large in people's lives.

So while we can be part of a place like Winscot Road from time to time, we are just visitors on its stage, which is more lasting than us or our possessions. We are just actors playing a small, short part in time's long play. And finally, the fading spotlight on our own existence is lost in the brightness of eternity as others go down life's long path to places like Winscot Road and fade into its rolling plains as we did that day.

Sunset Picnic in Aransas Park

One fine winter day, we went on a little picnic in the park by the house. It was something I had told you I wanted to do. We would sip on some wine, eat some finger foods, and watch the sunset, sitting on a blanket on the grass.

Late one afternoon, I packed the ice chest; and we drove down the hill to the middle of the park and walked to a spot we had picked out one day before when we were walking. We spread out the blanket, opened some wine, and watched the world go by as the sun neared the horizon in front of us. As the air started to cool we noshed on some food and watched people go by with their kids or their dogs. A few talked to us, said we had a good idea, and that they should do it, too.

Time went on, the sun did set, and the light started to wane. We sat there, talking to each other about nothing in particular; we just went from thing to thing for no reason at all. We were simply alive and enjoying what was before us that cool, sunny day.

And perhaps that is the point. Sometimes to be more alive, we have to simply live and not always "do." We had a great time on a little knoll covered with grass near a creek in a park. There was nothing fancy or lavish about it at all, but it was a grand thing to do. It was uncomplicated and fun with no pressing agenda to hurry us about. But it was still something worth remembering.

So when I walk past there now, the afterglow of that simple, yet meaningful time, lingers in my mind. I can still see us on the blanket by the

Notes to Stephanie: Days Remembered

trees in the dimming light; the image remains crystal clear. Thus, the memories of such times can last well after they happened and touch our heart and soul.

Jeffery W. Turner

I Wish We Had...

Do you recall the night I cooked you dinner and we watched the movie *Pure Country* starring George Strait? That movie always appealed to me since it showed aspects of our western culture and was filmed in and around Fort Worth, Maypearl, and Cresson.

The scenes around Fort Worth and Cresson were especially interesting to me since they were shot at places I had been to like the Worthington Hotel and drove by each day like the farm house at Cresson. It was funny how a movie showed scenes not just from the script but also from our own lives.

The scenes around Maypearl, however, did not contain that familiarity since I had never been there. I knew where that little town was; but like a multitude of other such places, I had never been there. Since I had not seen it, except through the lens of the camera, I was curious about it. One specific place I wanted to visit was the honky tonk where some scenes were set.

The bar and dance hall scenes portrayed there were certainly familiar, having been to such places growing up to drink beer and chase girls on the weekends. It was unknown, yet fully recognizable in my mind. Seeing the tables and beer signs on the walls of the place, I pictured us there dancing on the old wooden floor and sipping cold, longneck beers like they had in the movie. In a way, going there would have made our own movie, dancing the night away and loving on each like couples are shown doing in country western films. But we never did that. And I wish we had.

In *Pure Country*, George Strait's lifetime buddy recounts a childhood story where they spied a carnival proprietor who had a "dancing chicken." Unbeknownst to the people watching, the poor bird was scooting around frantically because the surface he was on was being heated by a concealed stove beneath it. George and his friend laughed about that and his friend asked, "Why didn't the chicken just jump off of the stage?" George replied that he didn't know and sometimes he felt like the chicken since many things were out of his control. He thought about "just jumping off" to get away from it all. In the movie, he did jump off of the busy stage and pursued things he felt he had lost on the way to finding success.

Thinking back over a lot of things, we should have jumped off the stage, drove down to Maypearl, and danced the night away. Such a night of fun and fantasy might have turned down the heat turning up on us and would have provided some welcome relief.

If we had done that more often, especially when things between us were tense, our own movie might have had a different ending—one more like the one George Strait and his leading lady had.

If only… if only… if only, we had just jumped off the stage like George Strait did that day.

Notes to Stephanie: Days Remembered

Do You Remember?

Do you remember our CERT class graduation exercise when I drafted you as my "buddy" to see who was "hurt" and who was "dead"?

Do you remember when I tried to teach you to dance, so we could go dancing one night?

Do you remember our wedding party? Devoid of my family, but we had yours and our friends?

Do you remember eating breakfast at Dos Molinas? The taste of menudo, barbacoa, and a beer?

Do you remember the time we ate goat on Seminary Drive, and it wasn't so good?

Do you remember Toby the **kitten** flying through the air from the game room upstairs into my arms?

Do you remember eating BBQ at Railhead and Angelo's with a couple of beers? Eating Indian buffet after church and gorging at Taco Palinque and the Turkey Shop, too?

Notes to Stephanie: Days Remembered

Do you remember your son in the ER and mine so sick in the ICU?

Do you remember shopping for a car? Looking at Hondas, Toyotas, Saturns, and more and buying the Camry you named Miss Precious and held so dear?

Do you remember moving your son? Loading up the truck and carting his stuff?

Do you remember how I listened to you when you had a hard time at school?

Do you remember cuddling so close at night in the bed to keep us both warm?

Do you remember going to garage sales on Saturdays and how I was bored?

Do you remember how we doted over each other when we were sick or felt bad?

Do you remember the time we took a bubble bath in the tub? Some suds, some drinks, and then some love?

Do you remember how we talked on the phone on the way to work and on the way home, too?

Do you remember buying that concrete fairy for the front door, and Jimmy and I laughing at all of the stuff there?

Do you remember the sets of Dickens books I gave you that you read in bed?

Do you remember buying those pots for plants to go by the front door?

Notes to Stephanie: Days Remembered

Do you remember having a Coors Light with lime and some salt in the pool?

Do you remember how we got the oil changed on the car and the truck, keeping Lord Grey and Miss Precious happy and running so smooth?

Do you remember worrying about Jimmy in the middle of the night and going to see if he was okay?

Do you remember walking through Half Price Books on many a day?

Do you remember going to the Greek food festival in Dallas and the one in Fort Worth, too?

Do you remember going to the Main Street Art Festival and swimming through the crowds?

Do you remember how I made you waffles for breakfast and other good things, too?

Do you remember going to the school on Saturdays while I watched you work?

Do you remember hanging our clothes on the line between the trees to dry?

Do you remember taking walks in the park after dinner?

Do you remember how we held hands when we sat in Unity Church?

Do you remember when you bought me house shoes that I did not want to wear?

Do you remember the rocking chair you bought me at the garage sale near the house?

Notes to Stephanie: Days Remembered

Do you remember your son's troubles with cars and the "Last Ride" of my old Ford?

Do you remember eating cold water melon in the pool on a hot summer day?

Do you remember…?

Do you…?

Do…?

…?

Do you remember the days when we thought we were right? Days full of wonder, days without strife? Days when only love cast its bright light?

Jeffery W. Turner

Do you remember the days when we were one? Days now just remembered and gone? I remember those days; I guess you do, too.

Afterword

There, I have done it—written a book I never thought I would write. Suffice to say, it was easier than *NTS* in one way since the first draft took less time to complete (two weeks). In another way, it was harder, since I had changed and edited the content of this book for quite a long time until I produced the feel I wanted with the Notes and pictures inside. While there are more things I could write Notes about, I have said it all now about "Stephanie" and me.

Outside of the mechanics of writing this book, I think I have continued to paint a picture of life that most people can identify with. However, as I stated in the foreword, I chose to write mostly about the good days Stephanie and I had as opposed to the days that were not so good, although you can see a touch of sadness in my words sometimes as I looked back on certain things. Finally, I won't write about our relationship woes—nothing good would be served by doing that, although you can see hints of those times in Notes like "I Wish We Had…"

Regardless of my view of life or philosophies of existence, I hope this second batch of *Notes to Stephanie* brought you an interesting and enjoyable read, filled with things from married life. Maybe they will make you think of your own ***days remembered***, perhaps now half forgotten but still waiting to touch your heart once more.

Jeffery W. Turner

Special thanks in no particular order to Ruby, Jenn, Lynn, Margo, Mac, Don, Bennie, and Elaine for their help, support, advice, and editing of this work.

Notes to Stephanie: Days Remembered

For more information on the pictures in the book, please visit my gallery at:

http://www.redbubble.com/people/jeffturnerphoto

Upcoming Books:

I am working on two more books containing Notes:

Notes To My Kids: Little Stories About Grown Up Kids. *This book will be Notes about when my kids were little and things from later times like their high school or college days.*

Notes About My Kin: Stories About Growing Up And Family. *This book will be about my childhood and how much my family meant to me as told through Notes with tales and stories from those times.*

No release dates are set for these two works. Together the four Notes books will be called "The Notes Series."